Daniel's Commentary

On Bible Prophecy

WestBow Press books may be ordered through booksellers or by contacting:

WestBow Press
A Division of Thomas Nelson
1663 Liberty Drive
Bloomington, IN 47403
www.westbowpress.com
1-(866) 928-1240

Because of the dynamic nature of the Internet, any web addresses or
links contained in this book may have changed since publication and
may no longer be valid. The views expressed in this work are solely those
of the author and do not necessarily reflect the views of the publisher,
and the publisher hereby disclaims any responsibility for them.

Any people depicted in stock imagery provided by Thinkstock are models,
and such images are being used for illustrative purposes only.

Certain stock imagery © Thinkstock.

ISBN: 978-1-4908-0593-1 (sc)
ISBN: 978-1-4908-0592-4 (e)

Library of Congress Control Number: 2013915115

Printed in the United States of America.

WestBow Press rev. date: 08/20/2013

WESTBOW
PRESS
A DIVISION OF THOMAS NELSON

Daniel's Commentary

On Bible Prophecy

by Daniel Ropp

Table of Contents

Table of Contents Continued

Introduction

This book is intended to address some of the more difficult prophetic passages that we encounter in Scripture. These commentaries primarily focus on end-time Bible prophecy and are not intended to be an exhaustive source for Bible prophecy. Neither is this a verse by verse study of the book of Revelation. This book has been designed to serve primarily as a reference source for anyone involved in a prophetic Bible study dealing with the end times.

I first began putting these commentaries in emails only to discover later that those receiving these commentaries were printing them off and saving them for future reference and study. That is when I realized I needed to compile them all in one book so they could be made available to anyone interested in the subject of end-time Bible prophecy. Why focus primarily on end-time Bible prophecy and not Bible prophecy in general? Because people want to know in what way the Bible is up-to-date right now and how these prophecies will affect them today, and what they can expect will happen tomorrow or in their life time. Secondly, people need to see that the Bible is relevant to the day in which we live right now and that makes it a living Book.

The scriptures quoted are from the NKJV unless otherwise noted. Other versions referenced are: NASV, KJV and the NIV.

The inspiration for this work has come from the Holy Spirit without which these commentaries would not have been made possible! I can never thank Him enough for the insight He has provided!

Chapter One
Veiled In The Patriarchs

In Genesis chapter five are listed the names of the patriarchs through which the Godly line was perpetuated until the flood and the time of Noah. Ten names are given: Adam, Seth, Enosh, Cainan, Mahalalel, Jared, Enoch, Methusaleh, Lamech and Noah.

The meaning of their names, unbeknown to them, would reveal the person-hood of Jesus and His salvation plan once He came to earth.

<u>Adam's</u> name means "ground." He was fashioned out of the dust and became flesh and was sinless initially. In Hebrews 10.5 it says this about Jesus, "...But a body you have prepared for Me..." meaning God had prepared Him to be the ultimate sacrifice. John 1.14 also says, "And the Word became flesh and dwelt among us..." And with regard to being sinless, 2Corinthians 5.21 says, "For He made Him who knew no sin to be sin for us that we might become the righteous of God in Him."

<u>Seth's</u> name means "substitute." It is well understood that Jesus is our substitute taking our sins upon Himself. Isaiah 53.4 says, "Surely He has borne our griefs and carried our sorrows; yet we esteemed Him stricken, smitten by God, and afflicted." And verse six goes on to say, "...And the Lord has laid on Him the iniquity of us all."

<u>Enosh's</u> name means "a man." Jesus frequently referred to Himself as the Son of Man. In Matthew 9.6 Jesus said, "...the Son of Man has power on earth to forgive sins.." In Matthew 16.13 Jesus said, "...Who do men say that I the Son of Man am?" And there are many more references to Him being the Son of Man.

1

<u>Cainan's</u> name means "fixed." Daniel 6.26 says, "...the God of Daniel... He is the living God, and steadfast forever..." Hebrews 13.8 says, "Jesus Christ is the same yesterday, today, and forever."

<u>Mahalalel's</u> name means "praise of God." Deut. 10.21 says, "He is your praise, and He is your God..." Psalm 48.10 says, According to Your name O God, so is Your praise to the ends of the earth..." And Psalm 106.2 says, "Who can utter the mighty acts of the Lord? Who can declare all His praise?" Yes our praise to Him is naturally inspired when we get a glimpse of His glory.

<u>Jared's</u> name means "a descent." Jesus said this about Himself in John 3.13, "No one has ascended to heaven, but He who came down from heaven, that is the Son of Man." In John 6.33 Jesus said, "For the bread of God is He who comes down from heaven and gives life to the world."

<u>Enoch's</u> name means "initiated." To break this down further it means to indoctrinate, enlighten, and to teach. Jesus was called Rabbi the great teacher and He did enlighten us and initiated a New Covenant in His blood. In John 6.45 Jesus said, 'It is written in the prophets, and they shall all be taught by God. Therefore everyone who has heard and learned from the Father comes to Me.'" Yes, the plan of salvation was initiated in Christ Jesus by the Father.

Genesis 5.24 also says, "Enoch walked with God; and he was not, for God took him." Enoch in this regard represents the true Church who also walks with God. Enoch was taken out <u>before</u> the flood came as will the Church be taken out before the great tribulation. Our relationship with Him is priceless!

<u>Methusaleh's</u> name means "man of a dart." Again this refers to Jesus.

2

John 19.34 says, "But one of the soldiers pierced His side, with a spear..." Zech. 12.10 says, "And I will pour on the house of David and on the inhabitants of Jerusalem the Spirit of grace and supplication; then they will look on Me whom they pierced..." And Rev.1.7 says, "Behold, He is coming with clouds, and every eye will see Him, even they who pierced Him..."

Lamech's name means "overthrower." Jesus overthrew the traditions of the religious leaders, the perception of who the people thought He should be, the tables of the money changers at the temple, false teachings of the Sadducees, cast out demons and defeated Satan at Calvary. In John 16.33 Jesus said, "...be of good cheer, I have overcome the world." 1John 3.8 says, "...For this purpose the Son of God was manifested, that He might destroy the works of the devil."

Noah's name means "rest." In Matthew 11.28 Jesus said, "Come to Me all you who labor and are heavy laden, and I will give you rest." And Hebrews 4.8-9 says, "For if Joshua had given them rest, then He would not afterward have spoken of another day. There remains therefore a rest for the people of God."

One might not think too much of the meaning of names except these are in a particular order necessary to follow the fulfillment of the unfolding plan of God. What is really important to see in all of this is to know and see how God is so deeply involved in the affairs of men even to the point of watching over the patriarchs in the giving of their names in an order that reveals who His Son would be as the intended Saviour of the world. Yes, we have looked behind the veil and lo and behold, we find our God has been there orchestrating it all.

Chapter Two
Predetermined 1948 End-Time Generation

This geneological table shows the derivation of the two one thousand nine hundred and forty eight year periods that have pointed to the 1948 end-time generation - the result which also reveals the third and last 1948 period establishing the significance of the 1948 generation spoken of by Jesus. The dates for this geneology are taken straight from scripture and since the Word of God is infallable these dates are therefore infallable.

Reference	Sequence	Years	Running Total
Gen. 5.3	Adam to Seth	130	
Gen. 5.6	Seth to Enosh	105	235
Gen. 5.9	Enosh to Cainan	90	325
Gen. 5.12	Cainan to Mahalalel	70	395
Gen. 5.15	Mahalalel to Jared	65	460
Gen. 5.18	Jared to Enoch	162	622
Gen. 5.21	Enoch to Methuselah	65	687
Gen. 5.25	Methuselah to Lamech	187	874
Gen. 5.28-29	Lamech to Noah	182	1056

Reference	Sequence	Years	Running Total
Gen. 5.32	Noah to Shem	500	1556
Gen. 11.10	Shem to Arphaxad	102	1658
Gen. 11.12	Arphaxad to Salah	35	1693
Gen. 11.14	Salah to Eber	30	1723
Gen. 11.16	Eber to Peleg	34	1757
Gen. 11.18	Peleg to Reu	30	1787
Gen. 11.20	Reu to Serug	32	1819
Gen. 11.22	Serug to Nahor	30	1849
Gen. 11.24	Nahor to Terah	29	1878
Gen. 11.26	Terah to Abram	70	**1948**
Gen. 21.5	Abram to Isaac	100	2048
Gen. 25.26	Isaac to Jacob	60	2108
See note on Jacob to Joseph	Jacob to Joseph	91	2199
Gen. 37.2, 28	Joseph to Egypt	17	2216
Ex. 12. 40-41	Jacob's descendants in Egypt to Exodus	430	2646
1Kings 6.1	Exodus to Solomon's reign	476	3122

Reference	Sequence	Years	Running Total
See Kings list Appendix 1	Solomon's reign to **Neb. takes captives to Bab.	414.25	3536.25
Ezra 1.1-3	Jews free to leave Babylon	70	3606*
Dan.9.25-26 Ezra 7.12-26	From decree to restore until Messiah is cut off	483	4089*

*Rounded off to the nearest year
**Nebuchadnezzar

So the time of Adam to the Messiah being cut off is 4089 years, but subtracting 33 years of Jesus' earthly time brings us to 4056 years i.e. from Adam to birth of Jesus. Now subtracting time of Adam to Jacob 2108 years from time of Adam to Jesus' birth 4056 years you get 4056 - 2108=**1948 years from Jacob (Israel) to Jesus' birth**. Then Jesus gave us the parable of the fig tree which pointed to the rebirth of Israel in **1948**. Only God could have made it work out like this which shows that the plan of God is still definitely in His control, and in 6,000 years Satan still has not been able to derail God's plan!

Notes on Jacob to Joseph

According to Genesis 37.2, 28 Joseph went to Egypt at 17 years of age and so he was the beginning of Jacob's descendents to go to Egypt. Then according to Genesis 41.40 Joseph was 30 years old when he began his regency under Pharoah. He sent for his family in Canaan to come to Egypt when he was 39 years old (Gen. 45.6) and Jacob was 130 years old when he stood before Pharoah (Gen.47.9). Therefore, Jacob was 91 years old when Joseph was born (130 - 39 = 91).

Chapter Three
The Restoration of God's People After The Babylonian Captivity

Understanding this will give us a good basis for when the 70 weeks of Daniel began as well as when Jesus was born. Daniel 9.25 is key here. It says, "Know therefore and understand that from the going forth of the command to <u>restore</u> and build Jerusalem until Messiah the Prince, there shall be seven weeks and sixty-two weeks..." This verse is addressing 69 of those 70 weeks.

There has been a lot of debate among scholars about just when the time clock started for the 70 weeks of Daniel. Those who used Nehemiah instead of Ezra missed the true starting point. Thus there has been a lot of manipulation of the numbers to try and get the years to fit. Once you focus on the main issue which wasn't the walls of Jerusalem you are able to solve the problem.

As far as God was concerned <u>restoration</u> of His people was the main issue all along and still is. You see God's people went into captivity because they had turned away from following God's commands. So now the important issue was to bring them back to Him through a spiritual restoration. Thus God moves on Ezra to bring this about in 451 B.C. One of the things we want to determine is how do we arrive at that date and then we will see why that date is important.

Analyzing passages from the book of Ezra will be our focus and one of the things of concern to us are the Persian kings that are necessary to the account and the timing. In chapter one is the Persian king Cyrus. In chapter four Ahasuerus and Artaxerxes and in chapters five and six, Darius and then Artaxerxes in chapter seven.

First of all, you may have noticed that Ezra mentions king Artaxerxes two different times - chapter four and chapter seven. The first question is, "Are they the same king?" The answer is no.

A very important clue makes this apparent. The Artaxerxes in chapter four verses 17-24 wrote a letter to be sent to the Jews in Jerusalem to stop their building there, but the Artaxerxes in chapter seven issued a decree to carry on the work of God in Jerusalem and provided gold and silver for the beautification of the temple and to buy animals for the sacrifices.

A little secular history helps to fill in on some interesting details. Cyrus as we know, was the Persian king (Ezra 1.1,3) who let the Jews - those who wanted to - go back to Jerusalem. Cyrus had a son named Cambyses who reigned after him for eight years. This Cambyses isn't mentioned in Ezra's account but he had a brother who is. He is mentioned as Artaxerxes in chapter four but that was only a title that he assumed; it wasn't his real name. This Artaxerxes was an imposter on the throne for seven months before Cambyses had him killed, and he was the one who had the work stopped in Jerusalem. We know Cambyses was off on a campaign to conquer Egypt which he did and while he was out of the country it may have been that this Pseudo Smerdis (Artaxerxes) assumed the throne at that time.

Persian kings chose titles according to how they wanted to be known. Darius for example, simply means "Doer of Good." Artaxerxes means "High King or Great King." It turns out, Darius used this title for six years after which he began using the title Artaxerxes. Further evidence of this is Ezra 6.14 where Darius and Artaxerxes is called king of Persia - not kings of Persia.

The scripture infers he aspired to greatness throughout his reign because by the time he gave Ezra a copy of the decree he had called himself "Artaxerxes king of kings"(Ezra 7.12). Again, another more lofty title.

Darius had already reigned six years when the temple was finished (Ezra 6.15) and sometime after this he began going by the title "Artaxerxes." It was seven years later that Ezra came to him to ask permission to go to Jerusalem and it was then that Artaxerxes announced the decree (Ezra 7.12-25) spoken of by the prophet Daniel. It was time to deal with the spiritual restoration of the people. So this would have been 13 years into the reign of the Persian king. It is a consensus among historical scholars that he began his reign in 464 B.C. Moving forward 13 years from that would have put the date at 451 B.C. when the clock began ticking for the 70 weeks of Daniel.

This date (451 B.C.) also provides additional information for when the birth of Christ took place. If you remember, Daniel 9.26 said, "And after the sixty-two weeks Messiah will be cut off..." And as we know, the sixty-two weeks represent the end of the 69 weeks or 483 years. But since 33 of those years represent Christ's time on earth they must be subtracted from 483 to see how many of those years had passed before Christ was born (483 - 33 = 450). As you can see 450 years had passed. But the clock started ticking for the 483 years in 451 B.C.

So Christ's birth then actually took place in what we would call 1 B.C (451 - 450 = 1 B.C.) as there is no year zero. This places the cutting off of the Messiah in 32 A.D. at which time the clock stopped at the end of the 69 weeks leaving one week of the 70 remaining to be fulfilled.

9

Chapter Four
The Scepter of Judah

For years I've wondered about the story of Jesus who went with His parents to Jerusalem for the Passover and then lingered behind to discuss Scripture with those rabbis in the temple when He was only 12 years of age. Now Jesus went with His parents every year to Jerusalem for the Passover but this year it was singled out for particular mention. The significance of this is monumental for Israel if I'm correct about this. I believe it very well could be related to the scripture in Genesis 49.10 that part of the verse which reads, "The scepter shall not depart from Judah, nor a lawgiver from between his feet until Shiloh comes..."

First of all, "Shiloh" is a crytogram for the Messiah so we know it is speaking about Jesus here. In the case of Israel "scepter" represented the authority the Sanhedrin had to legally mete out corporeal punishment. This authority was taken away from them around 11 A.D. by the Romans.

Now here is the dilemna for the religious leadership. They knew the scepter was not to be taken away from them until the Messiah had come but they didn't recognize that He had come so the dilemna was this - was their infallable Scriptures wrong? Once the scepter was taken away it was to be a sign to them that the Messiah had indeed come. Well we know Jesus was born in what we call 1B.C. as there is no year zero so in 11 A.D. Jesus would have been 12 years old, as the scripture says He was, when He was discussing the scriptures with the rabbis in the temple, but they didn't recognize Him for who He was.

So the dilemna still exists for Israel today meaning if they believe their Scriptures then they must believe the Messiah has indeed come.

Well if this wasn't enough evidence for them all the religious leadership had to do was wait until Jesus began His ministry officially when Jesus fulfilled the prophecy in Psalm 146.8. It says, "The Lord opens the eyes of the blind: the Lord raises those who are bowed down..." Prior to Jesus' ministry never had any of God's servants, messengers, prophets or priests ever opened the eyes of a blind person. Never!

Genesis 49.10 actually received a double fulfillment. In 70 A.D. when Jerusalem and the temple were destroyed by the Romans this should have removed any doubt that the scepter had departed from Judah, and any doubt about whether the Messsiah had come or not.

I find it fascinating and sad that none are so blind as those who choose to not see.

Chapter Five
Last Days of End Time Generation

I never ceased to be amazed at the significant events which have pointed to the 1948 generation. For example, Abram was born 1948 years after Adam, and Jacob whose name was changed to Israel was born 1948 B.C., and Jesus came into this world 1948 years after that. Then in 1948 A.D. Israel was reborn as a revived independent nation state, which was foretold in Jesus' prophecy through the parable of the fig tree. But what was Jesus giving us when He gave us the parable of the fig tree? Answer - It was timing! Yes, Jesus indicated we would recognize this particular generation in two ways. First, would be by Israel emerging as a nation state again, and second, by the events He mentioned that would take place in the world in that generation.

Jesus indicated the beginning events of this 1948 generation would be characterized by nation rising up against nation and kingdom against kingdom, and that this would be the beginning of birth pangs. Well just from 1948 until 2013 I counted a minimum of 70 wars of nation against nation, and 145 conflicts of kingdom against kingdom!

Jesus also mentioned that there would be other nation states that would emerge in the 1948 generation with Israel. Just since 1948 114 countries have declared nation state independence. I think this is significant because going back as far as 1579 there was one, the Netherlands, declaring its independence from Spain. Then it was almost 200 years before there was another when the U.S. declared its independence from the U.K.

I haven't mentioned the other things that Jesus said would take place in this same generation such as the seven year tribulation period and His return to reign over the earth but the important thing is Jesus said that "all" these things would happen in this same generation. Well, we are already 65 years into this generation so it doesn't leave much time for all the remaining events to be fulfilled.

I've come to the point of why I have written this. Luke 21.28 says that when these things begin to happen to look up because our redemption draws near. He didn't say that your time of trouble draws near but instead our redemption. That word "redemption" means "deliverance." Hebrews 9.28 reaffirms this verse when it says, "...unto them that look for Him shall He appear the second time without sin unto salvation"(KJV).

The completing of our salvation is when we receive our glorified bodies and are caught up to meet the Lord in the air. But this verse also implies that those who aren't looking for Him will not see Him when He returns at this point in time.

Luke 21.36 cements what Jesus wants us to understand. He says, "Watch therefore, and pray always that you may be counted worthy to escape all these things that will come to pass and to stand before the Son of Man." Jesus indicates that when we escape these things we will stand before Him. And where is Jesus during the tribulation events? He is in heaven, meaning, that is where His bride will be also in order to be standing before Him. Yes, our time of departure is near at hand.

Chapter Six
Nation States That Declared Independence Since 1948

Jesus indicated in Luke 21.29-31 that at the time Israel would emerge from a dormant condition to become a nation state that other nations would be declaring their independence as well. "Then He spoke to them a parable: Look at the fig tree, and all the trees. When they are already budding, you see and know for yourselves that summer is now near. So you also, when you see these things happening know that the kingdom of God is near." Since the fig tree represented the nation of Israel then the other trees must represent nations as well.

Independence	Country	Independence	Country
Jan.4, 1948	Myanmar	Apr. 27, 1960	Togo
Feb. 3, 1948	Sri Lanka	Jun. 26, 1960	Madagascar
May 14, 1948	Israel	Jun. 30, 1960	Congo (Zaire)
Jul. 19, 1949	Laos	Jul. 1, 1960	Somalia
Aug. 8, 1949	Bhutan	Aug. 1, 1960	Benin
Dec. 27, 1949	Indonesia	Aug. 3, 1960	Niger
Dec. 24, 1951	Libya	Aug. 4, 1960	Senegal
Nov. 9, 1953	Cambodia	Aug. 5, 1960	Burkina Faso
Jan. 1, 1956	Sudan	Aug. 7, 1960	Ivory Coast
Mar. 2, 1956	Morocco	Aug. 11, 1960	Chad
Mar. 20, 1956	Tunisia	Aug. 13, 1960	Central Africa
Mar. 6, 1957	Ghana	Aug. 15, 1960	Congo Repub.
Aug. 31, 1957	Malaysia	Aug. 16, 1960	Cyprus
Oct. 2, 1958	Guinea	Aug. 17, 1960	Gabon
Jan. 1, 1960	Cameroon	Sep. 22, 1960	Mali

Independence	Country	Independence	Country
Oct. 1, 1960	Nigeria	Oct. 4, 1966	Lesotho
Nov. 28, 1960	Mauritania	Jan. 31, 1968	Naura
Apr. 27, 1961	Sierra Leone	Mar. 12, 1968	Mauritius
Jul. 19, 1961	Kuwait	Sep. 6, 1968	Swaziland
Jan. 1, 1962	Samoa	Oct. 12, 1968	Equatorial Guinea
Jul. 1, 1962	Burundi	Jun. 4, 1970	Tonga
Jul. 1, 1962	Rwanda	Oct. 10, 1970	Fiji
Jul. 5, 1962	Algeria	Aug. 15, 1971	Bahrain
Aug. 6, 1962	Jamaica	Sep. 3, 1971	Qatar
Aug. 31, 1962	Trinidad & Tobago	Dec. 2, 1971	UAE
Oct. 9, 1962	Uganda	Dec. 16, 1971	Bangladesh
Dec. 12, 1963	Kenya	Jul. 10, 1973	Bahamas
Jul. 6, 1964	Malawi	Sep. 24, 1973	Guinea-Bissau
Sep. 21, 1964	Malta	Feb. 7, 1974	Grenada
Oct. 24, 1964	Zambia	Jun. 25, 1975	Mozambique
Feb. 18, 1965	The Gambia	Jul. 5, 1975	Cape Verde
Jul. 26, 1965	The Maldives	Jul. 6, 1975	Comoros
Aug. 9, 1965	Singapore	Jul. 12, 1975	Sao Tome & Principe
Sep. 30, 1966	Botswana	Sep. 16, 1975	Paupa New Guinea
May 26, 1966	Guyana	Nov. 25, 1975	Suriname
Nov. 30, 1966	Barbados	Nov. 28, 1975	Timor-Leste

Independence	Country	Independence	Country
Jun. 29, 1976	Seychelles	Jun. 25, 1991	Slovenia
Jun. 27, 1977	Djibouti	Aug. 9, 1991	Georgia
Jul. 7, 1978	Solomon Islands	Aug. 20, 1991	Estonia
Oct. 1, 1978	Tuvalu	Aug. 24, 1991	Ukraine
Nov. 3, 1978	Dominica	Aug. 25, 1991	Belarus
Feb. 22, 1979	Saint Lucia	Aug. 27, 1991	Moldova
Apr. 1, 1979	Iran	Aug. 30, 1991	Azerbaijam
Jul. 12, 1979	St.Vincent & the Genadines	Aug. 31, 1991	Kyrgyzstan
Jul. 30, 1980	Vanuatu	Sep. 1, 1991	Uzbekistan
Sep. 21, 1981	Belize	Sep. 8, 1991	Macedonia
Nov. 1, 1981	Antigua & Barbuda	Sep. 9, 1991	Tajikistan
Sep. 19, 1983	St. Kitts & Nevis	Mar. 1, 1992	Bosnia & Herzegovina
Jan. 1, 1984	Brunei	Sep. 21, 1991	Armenia
Oct. 21, 1986	Marshall Islands	Oct. 27, 1991	Turkmenistan
Nov. 3, 1986	Micronesia	Dec. 16, 1991	Kazakhstan
Mar. 11, 1990	Lithuania	Apr. 11, 1992	Serbia
Mar. 21, 1990	Nambia	Jan. 1, 1993	Slovakia
Mar. 27, 1990	Yemen	May 24, 1993	Eritrea
Jun. 25, 1991	Coatia	Oct. 1, 1994	Palau
		Jun. 3, 2006	Montenegro

Chart 1

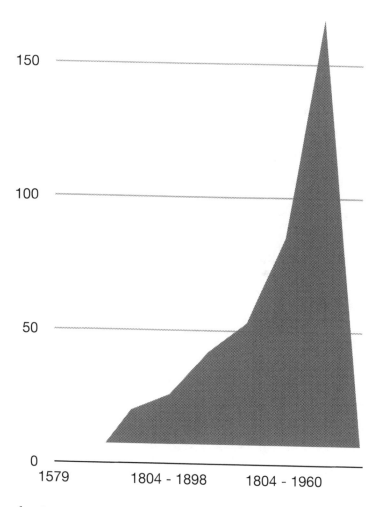

200			
150			
100			
50			
0			
1579	1804 - 1898	1804 - 1960	

Graph of nation states declaring their independence since 1579.
Notice how it spikes in the 1948 generation.

Chapter Seven
The Uniqueness of The Prayer of Moses

The prayer of Moses happens to be Psalm 90. So why is it in the book of Psalm at all since it was written by Moses about 400 years before the time of David? I think it was placed there so the reader would have a heightened sense of curiosity about its message An initial reading of the Psalm would seem to be a summary of the children of Israel's troublesome times. A closer reading would indicate the Psalm has prophetic overtones.

Moses' prayer addresses what he said in Deuteronomy 31.29. "For I know that after my death you will become utterly corrupt, and turn aside from the way which I have commanded you. And evil will befall you in the latter days, because you will do evil in the sight of the Lord, to provoke Him to anger through the work of your hands."

Knowing that His people would turn away, God entreats them, in Psalm 90.3, to return to Him because if they didn't they would have to face His anger (v.7). But we know Moses wasn't referring to his generation because Moses lived to be 120 years old and his brother Aaron to 123. Moses was instead referring to the typical life span of the latter day generation when he said in v. 10, "The days of our lives are seventy years; and if by reason of strength they are eighty years..."

Another thing that stands out in this Psalm is reference to God's wrath in verses 7, 9, and 11. This is interesting because this is how the 1948 end-time generation concludes by being subjected to God's wrath. Do the seal judgments, trumpet judgments and bowl judgments come to mind?

The tone of Moses prayer unexpectantly changes in verse 13 when he says, "Return O Lord! How long?..." Seeing that this Psalm is focused on the latter day generation this then must be pointing prophetically to the return of Jesus in the latter days. We realize this is the case when you notice that Moses <u>didn't</u> say, "come O Lord" as though waiting for Him to come the first time. Rather, Moses could only say prophetically, "return" if He had already come a first time.

Even the apostle John made note that the focus was not now upon Moses but upon Jesus as it was the beginning of a new dispensation. John 1.17 reads, "For the law was given through Moses, but grace and truth came through Jesus Christ."

Getting back to Moses' prayer, he recognized that the salvation, the deliverance, of God's people would only come from God because he went on to say in v.13, "...And have compassion on your servants," and in v.14, "Oh satisfy us early with Your mercy, that we may rejoice and be glad all our days!" In verse 17 Moses makes a crowning statement when he prays, "And let the beauty of the Lord our God be upon us..." This word "beauty" is a little bit unique in the Hebrew used only four times in the old testament and it links us to another scripture in Psalm 27.4 It reads, "One thing I have desired of the Lord, that will I seek: that I may dwell in the house of the Lord all the days of my life to behold the beauty of the Lord, and to inquire in His temple." You see this beauty is known only in the temple of the Lord. It is the next verse that ties all this together in v.5. It reads, "For <u>in the time of trouble</u> He shall hide me in His pavilion: <u>in the secret place of His tabernacle</u> He shall hide me; He shall set me high upon a rock."

19

This is even more clearly defined in Daniel 12.1 when it says, "...And there shall be a time of trouble such as never was a nation, even to that time. And at that time your people shall be delivered, every one who is found written in the book."

The prayer of Moses has indeed pointed us to our end time generation, to Christ who is to return for His people, and to a heavenly deliverance to His safe pavilion where we will behold His beauty and where we will be during the time of trouble (another term for the great tribulation).

I conclude this chapter with this verse in 1Corinthians 2.9. "But as it is written: 'Eye has not seen, nor ear heard, nor have entered into the heart of man the things which God has prepared for those who love Him.'"

Chapter Eight
Expectant or Unaware

These are two diametrically opposed concepts. I use these words with regard to the return of Christ for His Church - His bride. I believe Satan would rather people be unaware of when Christ will return and that he would perpetuate the idea that the time of Christ's return is unknowable so don't be concerned about it. On the other-hand Jesus would teach that we should be expectant of His return and would point out prophetic events for His people to be watching for so they would know when the time of His return was drawing near.

Satan is clever in promoting unawareness by having people quote Matthew 24.42. We are all familiar with this verse. "Watch therefore, for you do not know what hour your Lord is coming." He thinks he has a shut and closed case at this point. But we need to really stop and think about the words that Jesus is using here. Let's take the first word "watch." Does it make any sense to say watch to people who are already watching or to say watch to people who aren't watching? I get a little concerned about people who quote this verse because it makes me think they may have let their guard down.

It is important to look at the passage this verse was taken out of and the context of the passage. Jesus gave several examples here so let's look at the first one in verses 37-39. "But as the days of Noah were so also will the coming of the Son of Man be. For as in the days before the flood, they were eating and drinking, marrying and giving in marriage until the day that Noah entered the ark, and did not know until the flood came and took them all away, so also will the coming of the Son of Man be."

The main theme Jesus is addressing in this example is that society didn't believe Noah's message and his work was relevant to their day. They rejected the message to prepare themselves for the global change that was coming. Today society is choosing unconcern and irrelevance with regard to the Word of God as well.

Next, two examples are given of people working in the fields and at the mill where one is taken and the other is left. Then you come to the verse quoted earlier. "Watch therefore, for you do not know what hour your Lord is coming." This implies those who haven't been watching don't know, therefore, they are to watch. Jesus is saying don't be <u>unaware</u>! He goes on to say to those who are not ready to be ready. Verse 44 reads, "Therefore you also be ready, for the Son of Man is coming at an hour you do not expect." So when Jesus says "Be ready" it implies it is possible to be ready. It is expected!

Jesus did not come to call the righteous but sinners to repentance (Matt. 9.13) therefore, we need to keep in view the audience He is speaking to. He warns against being unaware. In Luke 21.34 He says, "But take heed to yourselves, lest your hearts be weighed down with carousing, drunkenness, and the cares of this life, and that Day come on you unexpectedly."

Maintaining our expectation will have its reward. "...To those who eagerly wait for Him He will appear a second time, apart from sin, for salvation." (Heb.9.28)

Chapter Nine
You Do Not Know The Day or The Hour

The following words are found in the last verse of the parable in Matthew 25: "Watch therefore, for you know neither the day nor the hour in which the Son of Man is coming" both in the KJV and the NKJV.   In the Alexandrian and Egyptian texts referred to as the NU - text, the words "in which the Son of Man is coming" are not there. So the NIV and the NASV do not have those words in that verse. Adding those words in the parable make the parable contradict itself. Why? Because of verses 6 and 7 which says, "But at midnight there was a shout, 'Behold, the bridegroom! Come out to meet him.' Then <u>all</u> those virgins rose and trimmed their lamps."

So it was well announced to the ten virgins that the bridegroom was coming. He just hadn't got there yet. Since it was well announced that the bridegroom was coming then it would make no sense to say "for you do not know the day or the hour in which the Son of Man is coming."

Let's leave those words "in which the Son of Man is coming" off that the NASV and NIV say shouldn't be there and what do we have? The NASV says, "Be on the alert then, for you do not know the day or the hour." One must ask, what is Jesus' intended meaning then of this parable? We have some clues.

First, who do the foolish virgins represent in todays society? They represent the religious church goer who has heard the stories in the Bible, call themselves Christians but never have had a born again experience. They are just religious having a form of Godliness.

So when they show up late to the wedding feast Jesus says to them, "Truly I say to you , I do not know you." Why didn't Jesus know them? Because they didn't have a relationship with Him, and that is key here to understanding this parable. Jesus is coming for a bride that He knows, one that has a relationship with Him.

This brings us to the meaning of the words in v.13. "Be on the alert then, for you do not know the day or the hour." The foolish virgins procrastinated - waited too long to get ready assuming they were ready or had plenty of time. But they didn't know how much time they would have before the door was shut. And this is what Jesus was implying to them that they wouldn't know at what day or hour the door would be shut to them.

Those who are not alert will not know, but those who are alert will know to be ready always.

Chapter Ten
Scriptural Evidence For A Pretrib Rapture

In the early 1970's when I was in Bible college one of the topics being debated was will there be a pretrib rapture, midtrib rapture or post-trib rapture? The Lord showed me the answer to this question, but I was surprised that the first scripture He referred me to was found in the old testament. That scripture was Isaiah 62.11-12. "Indeed the Lord has proclaimed to the end of the world: say to the daughter of Zion, 'Surely your salvation is coming; behold His reward is with Him, and His recompense accompanies Him.' And they shall call them the Holy People, the Redeemed of the Lord; and you shall be called Sought Out..."

So who is the Lord's recompense of v.11? His recompense is the Church, His bride whom He embraced after Israel had rejected Him. But in His return to Zion the verse says His recompense accompanies Him. This could only be possible if there had of been a prior rapture that united the Church with Him! Secondly, in v.12 they are identified as the Holy People, the Redeemed of the Lord as being a specific category of saints different from the people of Israel who the Lord identifies as the Sought Out ones. **This is our first witness.**

The book of Malachi was where I was directed next. In chapter four I noticed it spoke of the dreadful day of the Lord - a day designated for the ungodly and the wicked. My attention was directed to the end of chapter three to see what preceded it. Verse 16 says, "...So a book of remembrance was written before Him for those who fear the Lord and who meditate on His name."

Now God makes the following declaration in verses 17-18. "They shall be mine," says the Lord of hosts. On the day that I make them my jewels. And I will spare them as a man spares his own son who serves him. Then you will again discern between the righteous and the wicked, between one who serves God and one who does not serve Him." **This is our second witness.**

These verses reveal it isn't the saints who are able to save themselves from the coming time of tribulation but that it is an act of God that will do it. To make the case for a pretrib rapture to be more conclusive we turn to the book of 1Thessalonians. In chapter five and verses 9-10 we read: "For God did not appoint us to suffer wrath, but to obtain salvation through our Lord Jesus Christ, who died for us that whether we wake or sleep, we should live together with Him."

So where will we be if we are living together with Him? The last time I checked Jesus was in heaven at the right hand of the Father and the only way we are going to get there is by a heavenly translation. It is always good to have confirmation of this and we find it in chapter four verses 16 and 17. "For the Lord Himself will descend from heaven with a shout, of an archangel and with the trumpet of God, and the dead in Christ will rise first. Then we who are alive and remain shall be caught up together with them in the clouds to meet the Lord in the air. And thus we shall always be with the Lord. **This is our third witness.**

So yes, Malachi was right that we don't save ourselves but it will be through an act of God when Jesus calls us up.

Now let's look at the significance of the day of grace.

We all know that the word "grace" means unmerited favor. It is the apostle Paul who links the grace of God to a particular time period.

2Corinthians 6.1-2 says, "We then as workers with Him also plead with you not to receive the grace of God in vain. For He says: In an acceptable time I have heard you, and in the day of salvation I have helped you. Behold now is the time of My favor; behold, now is the day of salvation."

We have equivalent terms being used here i.e., an acceptable time, the time of My favor, and the day of salvation. Each one is inseperably linked to a time component. The Church today uses a little different term but it means the same to us when we mention the "age of grace." So the age of grace is the time of the Lord's favor.

Now we need to ask the question. What is the opposite of that? The opposite of that is known as the day of disfavor. Paul again says, in 1Thessalonians 5.5, "You are all sons of light and sons of the day. We are not of the night nor of darkness." So what follows the "day of favor" is the "day of disfavor" and we are not appointed to the "day of disfavor." The only way to escape the day of disfavor i.e. the tribulation period is by way of being translated out beforehand. **This is our fourth witness.**

Jesus addresses this in two places; the first being Rev.3.10. "Because you have kept My command to persevere, I also will keep you from the hour of trial which shall come upon the whole world, to test those who dwell on the earth." The word "from" in this verse means "out of" in the Greek. So the only way to keep us "out of" the hour of trial would necessitate a translation of the saints prior to it. **This is our fifth witness.**

27

Jesus also addresses the hour of trial or time of trouble in Luke 21.34-36. "But take heed to yourselves, lest your hearts be weighed down with carousig, drunkenness and cares of this life, and that Day come on you unexpectedly. For it will come as a snare on all who dwell on the face of the whole earth. Watch therefore, and pray always that you may be counted worthy to escape all these things that will come to pass, and to stand before the Son of Man."

So Jesus is saying it will be possible to escape all these things. Secondly, that after you've escaped these things you will be found to be standing before the Son of Man. And where is Jesus when all these things are happening on the earth? Revelation 6.1 says that Jesus is in heaven opening the seven seals. So the only way we could have gotten there is through a pretrib rapture. **This is our sixth witness.**

I believe any who deny the scripture's teaching on this do so at their own peril.

Paul in 2 Thessalonians 2.1 says, "Now we beseech you brethren by the coming of our Lord Jesus Christ and by our gathering together unto Him" (KJV).

Paul does not say, we entreat you, brethren by the coming of the day of the Lord. Rather, he said, "we beseech you, brethren, by the coming of our Lord Jesus Christ." Paul could only state this order of occurrence by being assured of its order, i.e. that the return of the Lord should be expected first. **This is our seventh witness.**

In 1Thessalonians 4.16 it reveals what takes place at the moment the translation of the saints takes place. Two things stand out. First, there is a voice from heaven and second there is a trumpet. Now when you get to Revelation 4.1 notice the similarity. "After these things I looked and behold, a door standing open in heaven. And the first <u>voice</u> which I heard was like <u>a trumpet</u> speaking with me, saying Come up here and I will show you things which must take place after this."

So it would appear in Revelation that John is representing the Church being caught up into heaven. This seems to be even more apparent when verse one says "after these things" at the beginning of the verse and "after this" at the end of the verse. Why is this significant? Because in chapters one through three the focus was entirely upon Church things. The implication is, that now we are finished dealing with the Church look at what follows. **This is our eighth witness.**

We are shown an interesting scene in heaven in verse 4. "Around the throne were twenty-four thrones, and on the thrones I saw twenty-four elders sitting, clothed in white robes; and they had crowns of gold on their heads." What do the 24 thrones and elders represent? They represent the 24 orders of the priesthood fulfilling the old testament type found in 1Chronicles 24.7-18. In Revelation 1.6 we see where the saints are made a kingdom of priests unto God. Therefore, since all 24 thrones are filled it means at this point in time all the priesthood (the Church) are present.

We have further confirmation of this. In Rev.4.4 they are all seen with crowns on their heads and the apostle Paul revealed that none of the saints would get their crowns until they all got them at the same time (2Timothy 4.8). This is further proof that the rapture has taken place at this point in time. **This is our ninth witness.**

We know the great tribulation time doesn't begin until the antichrist is revealed. He is seen for the first time in chapter six and verse two, but the crowned saints are seen in chapter four before the antichrist is revealed to the world in chapter six. The very sequence of these events, therefore, supports the rapture of the Church as being pretrib! **This is our tenth witness.**

Hebrews 9.28 indicates that only certain ones will see Him when He comes for His Church. "So Christ was once offered to bear the sins of many; and unto them that look for Him shall He appear without sin unto salvation"(KJV). This verse indicates Jesus does not appear to any unsaved people at this time but only to those who are ready and waiting for Him. It is important to see the Lord is not returning here to pour out His judgment or wrath; rather it is strictly for deliverance - the completion of our salvation, when we receive our glorified bodies and are delivered from this present evil age (Gal.1.4).

I had an experience years ago of what it will be like when the rapture takes place. I was fast asleep when all of a sudden I was awakened at 2 O'clock in the morning by the high pitched sound of a trumpet. It was a loud unwavering tone and it was moving across the sky. I wanted my wife to experience what I was experiencing so I woke her up and said, "Do you hear that sound of a horn?" And she said, "No I don't hear anything." I said, "I don't see how you can miss it." It was then I knew the experience was from the Lord not to teach my wife something but to teach me something. That was also when I realized born again Christians have a set of spiritual ears to hear with that those spiritually dead don't have activated. Jesus has certainly convinced me that the rapture will be as a thief in the night.

Significance of The Firstfruits

Jesus makes the following statement in John 10.16. "And other sheep I have which are not of this fold; them also I must bring, and they will hear My voice; and there will be one flock and one shepherd." Jesus was alluding to the Gentiles who would also come into the fold. They were represented as far back as one of the two wave loaves at the Feast of Weeks in Leviticus 23.16-17. "Count fifty days to the day after the seventh Sabbath; then you shall offer a new grain offering to the Lord. You shall bring from your dwellings two wave loaves...**They** are the first fruits to the Lord."

As you know this 50 day waiting period was given the title Pentecost and was fulfilled in the birth of the Church. The Church would be made up of two components - Jew and Gentile. It is important to remember that the Church is called the firstfruits to the Lord by the Lord Himself. Now let's move ahead in time to the apostle Paul and a statement he made in 1Corinthians 15.22-23 concerning the resurrections. "For as in Adam all die, even so in Christ all shall be made alive. But each one in his own order: Christ, the firstfruits, afterward those who are Christ's at His coming." So Paul here speaks of three separate resurrections: that of Christ, later the firstfruits (the Church) and later yet of those who would be resurrected at the return of the Lord when He is revealed to the nations.

Paul here is speaking specifically of the resurrections and their order and so the 144,000 are not mentioned here because they don't have a resurrection - they have a translation. Yes, the 144,000 are also called the firstfruits to God (Rev.14.4) representing the other wave loaf of Leviticus 23 presented to the Lord.

Now here is where it gets a little more interesting. The feasts as mentioned in Exodus and Leviticus were to be observed through future generations as a type that would find their fulfillment in future events. The Passover Lamb found its fulfillment in Christ when He died on the cross. The Festival of Firstfruits and the Feast of Ingathering both represent the first and the last of the good harvest times.

The Festival of Firstfruits will find its fulfillment soon in the rapture of the Church and the Feast of Ingathering will find its fulfillment in the rapture of the great tribulation saints for they are the last to come in before Jesus reigns on the earth for 1,000 years. The Feast of Ingathering took place in the Jewish 7th month at the time of the Feast of Tabernacles (Deut. 16.13). In both cases, for the Feast of Firstfruits and the Feast of Tabernacles there was to be a holy convocation. A holy convocation means an assembling of God's people together. This is precisely what happens at the time of the rapture of the Church (1Thess.3.13).

Holy convocations were to take place at their appointed times (Exodus 23.4). So if these feasts were required to be kept at their appointed time then the prophetic fulfillment of these will occur at their appointed time as well. Jesus fulfilled His part as the Passover Lamb at the precise time the former Passover observances were kept. This leads me to believe the other feasts will be fulfilled at their appointed times given in scripture. There is one other thing of interest here. Jesus' resurrection occured on the day of the Festival of the Firstfruits. Colossian 1.18 says, "And He is the head of the body, the Church..." So it would make sense that the Church being the body of Christ would also be raised on the day of the Festival of the Firstfruits and since this is also a festival of the harvest. I find this suspiciously interesting!

Chapter Twelve
The Feast of Unleavened Bread

The first clue as to what the Feast of Unleavened Bread is all about is found in the book of Departure, also better known as the book of Exodus. What we are looking at here are the establishment of types in the feasts that will be fulfilled at a later point in time.

With regard to the types, Egypt is symbolical of the world. Within Egypt were God's people as are God's people living in the world today. Though God's people were separate from the Egyptians they still lived among them and it parallels the lives of Christians in our world today God's people were in bondage in the sense that they were oppressed by the Egyptians and the same is true in many respects of Christians down through the centuries.

Now we need to look at a couple of things with regard to this feast in Exodus 12.15 and 17. [v.15] "Seven days you shall eat unleavened bread..." [v.17] "So you shall observe the Feast of Unleavened Bread, for on this same day I will have brought your armies out of the land of Egypt...."

Why eat it for seven days? It took that long to get all of God's people clear out of Egyptian territory. This feast also commemorated God's people being released from the oppression of the Egyptians. In fulfilling the type the seven days represents seven years. That seven years will parallel the seven years of trial or tribulation for the world only God's people, the Church, will have been delivered and will be living in peace in heaven during this time.

So why did the bread that they ate have to be unleavened? Unleavened bread represented the bread of humility.

All of God's people don't come in until the end of the seven years and those are known as the great tribulation saints and are represented as the last of the spiritual harvest in the Feast of Ingathering. Though the Feast of Unleavened Bread is meant to be a joyous time never-the-less within an atmosphere of humility.

The Lord gives additional information in Exodus 12.16. "On the first day there shall be a holy convocation and on the seventh day there shall be a holy convocation." In case one is wondering, a holy convocation is a meeting of all the saints that are present. All those that God will have delivered up to that point will be there. The Church are the firstfruits unto God that will be represented there which is further proof that there is a pretrib rapture. And then on the day of the Feast of Ingathering there will be another holy convocation as depicted in verse 16. Do you know why this is called a holy convocation? It is because the unholy won't be there!

It is interesting, that in verse 17 when the Feast of Unleavened Bread was to commence the Lord says, "...on this same day I will have brought your armies out of the land of Egypt..." But when the Lord returns to earth at the end of the seven years Rev. 19.14 says, "And the armies in heaven clothed in fine linen, white and clean, followed Him on white horses."

Timing? Well Exodus 13.3-4 bears quoting. "...Remember this day in which you went out of Egypt, out of the house of bondage; for by strength of hand the LORD brought you out of this place. No leavened bread shall be eaten. [v.4] On this day you are going out in the month Abib." Guess what? This is the same month in which the Feast of Firstfruits is celebrated (Ex.23.15-19). Coincidence?

Chapter Thirteen
Revealing Cherished Secrets

One might not think of the book Song of Solomon as containing any prophetic verses but chapter two intimates a prophetic voice. Verse one is a clue that there is something special to take note of when it says, "I am the rose of Sharon, and the lily of the valleys." Where have we seen those first two words before - "I am?" We saw them in Exodus 3.14. "And God said to Moses, I AM WHO I AM. And He said,, thus you shall say to the children of Israel, 'I AM has sent me to you.'" So the typology of the first verse ("I am the rose of Sharon") reveals this is speaking of Jesus.

In Revelation chapter 22 the words "I am" are used five times and three of those are associated with the phrase "I am coming quickly."

In Song of Solomon chapter two and verse four we realize there is a love affair taking place between Jesus and His bride to be. "He brought me to the banqueting house, and His banner over me was love." Yes, she arrives at a very special place.

Beginning in verse 8 we see some of the specifics of how this took place and when. I won't quote verses 8 and 9 but the gist is that when Jesus came, He came quickly. And then in v.10 we get to the "how" it happened. "My beloved spoke, and said to me: Rise up, my love, my fair one and come away." Does this remind you of what takes place at the rapture? 1Thessalonians 4.16 says, "For the Lord Himself will descend from heaven with a shout with the voice of an arch angel..." and we shall be caught up.

In Song of Solomon 2.14 we see why it was easy for Jesus to select His bride-to-be to go away with Him. "O my dove, in the clefts of the rock..." She was already found to be abiding in the Rock. Jesus Himself, said in Matthew 16.18 that He is the Rock that His Church would be established upon.

The next line of verse 14 I think is translated better in the KJV. It reads, "...in the secret places of the cliff in the NKJV, but in the KJV it reads, "...in the secret of the stairs." Where did we encounter the secret of the stairs before? It was Genesis 28.12 and 17 where Jacob saw in a dream a ladder going from earth to heaven with the angels ascending and descending on it, and Jacob when he awoke said, "..this is the gate of heaven."

Once this secret corridor is traversed we see in Song of Solomon 2.14 what the expectation of the bride-to-be is. "...Let me see your face, let me hear your voice..."

Verses 11-14 reveals the timing of the year this love encounter takes place. "For lo, the winter is past, the rain is over and gone, the flowers appear on the earth; the time of singing has come, and the voice of the turtledove is heard in our land. The fig tree puts forth her green figs and the vines with the tender grapes..."

I think it is obvious the time of year it is referring to is the spring. But we are given some specifics. The rain is over in the month of April - the turtledove is migratory and returns to Israel as early as mid April - the fig tree puts forth the taqsh, the early fig from late March to April. The NKJV says the vines are producing the tender grapes but this is a poor translation because the vines are actually blossoming and that is where this fragrance is coming from as indicated in the NASV. The point is, the vines also blossom in early spring.

37

It might interest you to know that the spring activity just mentioned occurs in the Jewish month of Abib which just happens to be in the same month of harvest as the Feast of Firstfruits (Exodus 23.15-16).

At the end of the time detailed in verses 11-13 these words are repeated, "...Rise up, my love, my fair one and come away!"

Chapter Fourteen
Fine Tuning Prophetic Sequences

As you know Daniel's 70th week - that last seven years which has been postponed due to Israel's rejection of Christ and which ushered in the Church age is going to command a lot of attention before long. Recently my attention was drawn to the two witnesses of Revelation 11. They will be witnessing in Israel during the first part of the 70th week.

If one were to draw a time line and mark it off in seven equal increments each representing a year this would depict the 70th week or seven year tribulation period. Anytime in the fourth year it would be considered the middle of the seven year period. So what event starts the time clock for this seven year period? If you say it is Jesus opening the first of the seven seals allowing the rider on the white horse to be revealed you are right. Now what ends or stops the clock for the seven year period? If you say, according to Daniel 9.24 that it is after Jesus comes back with His saints and is anointed by the high priest in Jerusalem with the special anointing oil to be King of Israel you would be correct again.

It is important to establish end points for the 70th week. Jesus takes rightful and legal claim to the throne of David when He is anointed King by the high priest. This priest will likely be among those who flee into the wilderness for 1260 days until it is safe to return to Jerusalem. Since 1260 days is equal to 3 1/2 years we know the Jews flee to the wilderness in the middle of the seven year period. Now we come to a scripture that is really central to our understanding here and it is Daniel 12.11.

It says, "And from the time that the daily sacrifice is taken away, and the abomination of desolation is set up, there shall be one thousand two hundred and ninety days." So if you count back from the end of the seven year period 1,290 days you arrive 30 days before the 3 1/2 year point is reached where the sacrifices are stopped. This brings us back to the two witnesses I mentioned at the first. You see Satan isn't completely stupid. He knows Bible prophecy just like we do at least to a point. The two witnesses were given power for the duration of the 1260 days of their ministry to kill their enemies by fire (Rev. 11.3-5). Satan isn't about to let his key player go up in smoke so he waits until he knows the days of their ministry has ended before he kills the two witnesses and then he can stop the sacrifices without being opposed by them.

Now here is where it gets interesting. You see the two witnesses were killed just before the sacrifices were stopped which was 30 days before you get to the 3 1/2 year point of the seven year period. But the two witnesses were given a ministry of a full 3 1/2 years or 1260 days. So the question is, when did their ministry start? Their ministry must start at least 30 days before the antichrist is revealed just before the 70th week begins.

This tells us the two witnesses appear on the world scene before the antichrist does - before the tribulation begins. It looks a little suspicious that the two witnesses arrive in Israel just after the rapture of the Church to begin witnessing because the Church won't be here to do it.

Chapter Fifteen
The Two Witnesses Ministry

In a previous commentary regarding the two witnesses I mentioned that after they were killed the time of "Jacob's trouble" would begin. Jacob's trouble was prophesied in Jeremiah 30.7, and also Daniel 12.1. The angel speaking to Daniel said, "...And at that time your people shall be delivered, every one who is found written in the book." The angel isn't talking about all Israel here but a specific group from within Israel namely those who've had their names written in the book.

This is the result of the ministry of the two witnesses and the converts they won to Christ. How many did they win? They won 144,000 over the course of their 3 1/2 year ministry. It appears the focus of their ministry was on the youth because in Malachi 4.5-6 it says, "Behold I will send you Elijah the prophet **before** the coming of the great and dreadful day of the Lord. And he will turn the hearts of the fathers to the children and the hearts of the children to their fathers..." This would also lend some support to why the 144,000 were virgins. Concerning the 144,000 Revelation 14.4 says, "These are the ones who were not defiled with women for they are virgins...These were redeemed from among men being firstfuits to God and to the Lamb."

These were new believers in the Lord - not seminary trained ministers evangelizing the world. There is no scripture saying these went through out the tribulation evangelizing. They are not even on the earth for the last 3 1/2 years of the tribulation. Proof of this can be found in Revelation chapter 14.

The sequence of events in chapter 14 is, first: the 144,000 standing before the throne of God (v.3), second; in verse 9 the angel warns the people on earth not to take the mark of the beast and the mark of the beast is not required until the beginning of the last half of the tribulation period. But according to the sequence of events the 144,000 are already in heaven before the throne of God.

If these 144,000 had had their names written in the Lamb's Book of Life prior to the beginning of the tribulation they would have gone up in the rapture with the rest of the Chruch. Their salvation at this time is a sign to the rest of Israel to take the prophecies of Scripture seriously. The remaining non-Messianic Jews finally get their eyes opened and bolt for the wilderness where they receive miraculous provision from God for the next 3 1/2 years (Rev. 12.6).

So what I see is the peace Israel experiences during the first 3 1/2 years of the tribulation can be attributed to the presence of the two witnesses in Israel. The antichrist will be kept at bay there until their ministry is completed.

Chapter Sixteen
Rebuilding The Jerusalem Temple

We know the scripture indicates the temple will be built again in Jerusalem in this 1948 generation (Matt. 24.15; 2Thess.2.4), but the question is when? The big question has been, will the temple be built before the tribulation begins or after it begins? I think we have enough evidence from scripture to be able to say the Church will not be here for the building of the Jerusalem temple.

One big clue comes from Daniel 9.27 where the antichrist confirms the covenant with Israel. There is no opposition to confirming this covenant because of a temple probably because it doesn't exist yet. But a little less than 3 1/2 years later we see strong opposition to the altar sacrifices by this same antichrist.

It is becoming increasing obvious that the Jews plan to build their temple on the temple mount probably just north of the Dome of the Rock. We have an inference to this from Rev.11.2 which says, "Leave out the court which is outside the temple, and do not measure it, for it has been given to the nations...." (NASV). Does the idea of Jerusalem being declared an international city ring any bells? So if there isn't room for the court of the Gentiles it is probably because the temple is situated too close to the Dome of the Rock.

Now here is where it gets interesting. The Jewish Sanhedrin considers that area of the temple mount to have been made unclean due to all the events that have transpired there over the centuries and therefore it must be cleansed before any building can commence. Therefore, they will build an altar for sacrifices before any building is allowed. We have a scriptural precedent for this.

When the Babylonian Jews returned from Babylon, before they started building the temple again, they first build an altar for burnt offerings (Ezra 3.2,6).

We must now go to Daniel 8.13-14 to complete the picture here. It reads, "...How long will the vision be, concerning the daily sacrifices and the transgression of desolation, the giving of both the sanctuary and the host to be trampled underfoot?" And he said to me, "For two thousand three hundred days then the sanctuary will be cleansed." This period is equivalent to 6 years, 4 months, and 19.5 days.

Since this is ocurring in the seven year tribulation period we must subtract the 6 years, 4 months, and 19.5 days from seven years to find out when they begin offering sacrifices. And our answer is 7 months and 10 days transpire from the start of the 70th week before they begin offering sacrifices. Therefore, the implication is they don't begin building the temple until shortly after this in the first year of the 7 year period of the tribulation.

It is interesting that this temple will also be built in troublesome times as was the one in Ezra's time (Dan. 9.25; Ezra 4.4...).

Chapter Seventeen
Mystery Babylon The Great Identified

In the book of Revelation chapter 17 we find what could be described as a prophetic parable revealing unique criteria that points to the identification of Mystery Babylon. The <u>key</u> to understanding chapter 17 is to view it as paranthetical. We need to understand it does not focus on a new sequence of events as though continuing from chapter 16. You see, in the chapters <u>prior</u> to chapter 17 John has been shown the seal judgments, the trumpet judgments, and by the time you get to the end of chapter 16 the bowl judgments. Now that the judgment events have been decreed, the angel begins to show John <u>additional</u> information that focuses on Mystery Babylon in particular.

General Timing. One of the secrets being revealed to us, in chapter 17, is that there are to be two phases to the judgment events upon Mystery Babylon the Great. We will find as we examine the text that the first phase of judgment begins before the Great Tribulation period commences. So this message is very relevant to us now! The second judgment occurs under the 7th bowl judgment. We begin by looking at verse one and verse five.

"Then one of the seven angels who had the seven bowls came and talked with me, "Come, I will show you the judgment of the great harlot who sits on many waters." [V.5] And on her forehead a name was written: MYSTERY BABYLON THE GREAT, THE MOTHER OF HARLOTS AND OF THE ABOMINATIONS OF THE EARTH."

So we wouldn't miss it, her name was inscribed on her forehead in capital letters, "MYSTERY BABYLON THE GREAT." As it turns out this is a metonym for America.

The word "MYSTERY" in the Greek here, means secret communiques that are religious and political in nature, passed down through secret protocol. There is a strong inference from this that those controlling the strings of government in the past as well as at the time of this judgment are involved with secret protocol. That means there are those appointed in government positions who have a different allegience than to the Constitution of the United States. An example would be the people who are members of the Council on Foreign Relations whose real aim is for a one world government, and to get there one must find ways to get around the Constitution.

We now come to another even more important identifier. The word "GREAT" in "BABYLON THE GREAT" in the Greek, is "mega" and means SUPER. This indicates **this end-time Babylon** will be known as a super entity or super power to the world just before she is judged. <u>If there is any one thing which identifies America here, it is this</u>! The little partially restored Babylon in Iraq does not fit this description, nor does the Vatican or Rome. In fact, this identifier rules out just about every nation but America. America is a super power among nations. Here is an example just from the perspective of defense spending alone. To quote the New American Investor, the 2004 summer issue, it stated: "the United States will spend more on defense than what Russia, China, U.K. France, Germany, Japan, South Korea, Australia, and India will spend on defense combined!" That statement helps to put America in perspective as a super power!

In verse one, the harlot is described as one who "sits on many waters." This is symbolism, which describes a nation made up of immigrants as America indeed is.

These identifiers are unique in that **all** of them fit the description of America and more will be given to us as we go through this chapter.

America is presently in a decline phase that precedes the judgment phase. The following list of events should make this apparent. In March of 2001 there was a pronounced downturn in the economy that caused bankruptcies of large corporations and <u>hundreds of thousands </u>of layoffs. Then in September terrorist attacks caused the collapse of the World Trade Center, considerable destruction at the Pentagon, and the anthrax mail problem. In 2002 there were massive fires in Arizona (spread out over 50 miles in length), the 500,000 acre Biscuit fire in the Siskiyou National Forest, and severe flooding in the Midwest. In 2003 there were serious blackouts in nine states and Canada followed by hurricane Isabel (one of the worst to hit the East coast in years), also noticeable devaluation of the dollar, and the destruction of roughly 3200 homes by fire in California. These are not just the typical house fire. Let me give a brief quote from Parade Magazine, the June issue of 2004. The article stated: "At first it was a crimson glow on the night horizon. soon ash began to fall - eerie, like snow - then bits of flaming brush. Small fires flared up beside the house. And then came an ominous rumbling - the sound of a massive wild fire on the move, shaking the earth, leaping into the tops of drought stricken oaks. A roiling mass of smoke descended. And then it hit, a 100 foot wall of wind-driven flame hurtling out of the night, moving as fast as 2 acres per second. The rumbling became a roar, became terror, became death itself."

Beginning in March of 2004 we saw fuel prices take a dramatic increase at the gas pump. Airline fares were also affected because of this.

Then in 2005 there were hurricanes Katrina, Wilma, and Rita leaving over $115 billion dollars in damages and over 1500 lives lost. In 2006 the housing bubble began collapsing, and in 2007 the U.S. dollar dropped to a new low against the Euro and the housing bubble continued its downward slide. In 2008 large megabanks began declaring huge losses. This resulted in several large bank mergers. For example, Washington Mutual was the largest bank failure in U.S. history and was taken over by Chase bank. In this same year there was also hurricane Ike leaving $19.3 billion dollars in damages and 103 deaths. There was also a swarm of fierce tornadoes that swept across the midwest. Auto companies GM and Chrysler required bailouts to keep solvent. In 2009 unemployment went from 5.8% to over 10% and in 2010 there has been the worst oil spill in the Gulf in America's history.

In 2011 a deranged shooter in Arizona killed six people and severly wounded Congresswoman Giffords. A very rare 5.8 earthquake hit the East coast and a deadly tornado hit Joplin Missouri killing over 100 people. In 2012 hurricane Sandy hit the East coast and was the second most costly storm in U.S. history. This is also the year Americans re-elected a President who has run up the national debt to over 16 trillion dollars. In 2013 Colorado has lost over 400 homes to wild fires.

In 2001 regular unleaded gas was selling for $1.00 a gallon and in 2013 for $3.45 a gallon. Diesel was selling for $.91 a gallon and in 2013 for $3.79 a gallon. So there is a visible downward trend over the last several years of serious economic troubles and it isn't getting any better. A more serious encompassing judgment will follow this decline phase.

God does not want America to go through terrible judgment. This is why the chastising events have been very measured up until now. God keeps looking for repentant hearts so He can mitigate the judgment, but what He is finding is increasing rebellion against Him. This has been apparent through an increasing corrupt judicial system, perversion expressed in Hollywood films and actors, the bias in the media against morality, inequality of justice, and distaste in our public education system for acknowledging God and His role in our society just to name a few examples. Let's look now at verse three.

"So he carried me away in the Spirit into the wilderness. And I saw a woman sitting on a scarlet beast which was full of names of blasphemy, having seven heads and ten horns."

Here the harlot is mentioned as as a woman sitting on a scarlet beast. The words that describe her as "sitting" on the beast shows she has chosen to associate herself with the beast, and in return the beast is giving her its support temporarily. For a while there is a mutually agreed relationship between them, but this will change. In this verse, not only do we find her sitting on the beast but she is also in a wilderness, i.e., she has found herself to now be in an uncultivated and uncultured environment. So what we are looking at here is America **after** she has gone through her decline phase and has started into her judgment phase.

Now verse four stresses the spiritual condition of the woman showing how depraved she has become. It says, "The woman was arrayed in purple and scarlet, and adorned with gold and precious stones and pearls, having in her hand a golden cup full of abominations and the filthiness of her fornication."

The fact that she is holding a cup made of gold reveals how much she cherishes what has been put into it. It is also clear that she has been a participant of what is found to be in the cup, which is abominations and filth of her fornication.

Abominations mean that which is detestable to God. For example, abortion is an abomination to God. The woman has come to a point where she has no shame. Her fornication is not hidden because the filthiness of it can be seen. Fornication here represents moral depravity and the pursuit of selfish gain. Now let's look at a very profound and sobering statement made in verse six.

"I saw the woman drunk with the blood of the saints and with the blood of the martyrs of Jesus. And when I saw her, I marveled with great astonishment." The word "marveled" here in the Greek means astonished or flabbergasted - in this case that there were martyrs of Jesus found in America. Think about that. Severe persecution will come to America. In our present day we are beginning to see more resistance against Church beliefs and it is even sanctioned through some government controlled entities. This isn't the end of the story as in the second judgment phase God will repay those persecutors big time.

It is easy to see now why the cup the woman was holding was so full of abominations and the filth of her fornication. She simply allowed any semblance or reference to God to be purged from public life. Eventually, (under the occupation, which I haven't really touched on) most Christian influence will be forcibly suppressed and martyrdoms will follow as the scripture has already indicated in verse six. Later in this chapter the angel will provide some more information that will put a better perspective on what is happening here.

Directing our attention to verse 7 and the first part of verse 8 the angel says, "Why did you marvel? I will tell you the mystery of the woman and of the beast that carries her, which has the seven heads and the ten horns. The beast that you saw was and is not, and will ascend out of the bottomless pit and go to perdition."

This beast is a bit of a mystery itself because it **has two aspects to it.** The first aspect of it is a spirit that is demonic in its nature. We know this because the verse says it ascends out of the bottomless pit. This spirit of Satan will be the spirit controlling this beast. Secondly, he will eventually possess an ungodly human vessel when the right time comes to do this. The one who will be known as the antichrist will be this indwelt person.

So for the moment, the beast that John sees is representing past kingdoms, the one present in his day, and a future one as this spirit of Satan has been active in every age. We know this because of the seven heads of the beast that also represent seven kings. The angel says in verse 10, "Five have fallen, one is and the other has not yet come." This definitely confirms that only the demonic spirit aspect of the beast could and does span the great time periods involved here.

I believe this demonic spirit has been previously identified in Revelation 12.3 and verse 9. There it says, "Another sign appeared in heaven: behold a great fiery red dragon having seven heads and ten horns, and seven diadems on his heads. [V.9] So the great dragon was cast out, that serpent of old, called the Devil and Satan, who deceives the whole world he was cast to the earth, and his angels were cast out with him."

You notice that this dragon (just as in Rev.17.3) has seven heads and ten horns, but it is specifically called Satan here.

51

The beast is described as fiery red like scarlet, just as the beast was shown to be in Rev. 17.3. So Satan is being represented in this way to show us that he was the one who influenced world kingdoms in ages past, and who it is that will affect the judgment to come on America, and what the end result of that influence will end up being.

In Revelation 17.8 when the angel says that the beast will ascend out of the bottomless pit and go into perdition he doesn't mean that Satan is there now. Rather, <u>the angel is revealing a terminating event</u> that will, at the appointed time, cut off his authority and ability to influence mankind on the earth. Rev. 20.7-9 reveals at the conclusion of the 1,000 year reign of Christ that Satan then comes out of the bottomless pit and tries to initiate the final battle of Gog and Magog. He miserably fails after which he is cast into the Lake of Fire (v.10).

The biggest mystery about the beast is when the angel (in Rev.17.8) says, "...the beast that was, and is not, and yet is." **The angel is speaking of already knowing what the final outcome is.** The outcome is probably not fully evident to John about what has just been said to him but to the angel the outcome is the same as being already accomplished.

Let's look at this in another way. If we describe the beast where each of its heads represent world empires it should bring some clarification. In verse 10 the angel reveals five of the seven world empires had already fallen in history and John was living in the sixth. The Roman empire, the sixth one, would be divided into East and West, the division becoming the mortal wound that would contribute to its demise. Knowing that this would happen the angel declares that it "is not."

A seventh head, or king is left to emerge in the **end-time** that we understand will be of relatively short duration. This seventh head is believed to be emerging from the European Union of nations that were formerly a part of the old Roman empire. It is forming the core of the last day empire that will throw its support behind the antichrist.

We come to another point of interest in verse 8. It reads, "And those who dwell on the earth will marvel, whose names are not written in the Book of Life from the foundation of the world, <u>when they see the beast</u>..." Pause just a moment. Did you notice that **those observing and marveling at the beast are the lost (those whose names are not written in the Book of Life)?** They are the only ones marveling at the beast. The saints are conspicuously absent! We will see why before we get to the end of the chapter. In the mean time, we are provided even more information to help identify the woman in verse 9. It says, "Here is the mind which has wisdom. The seven heads are seven mountains on which the woman sits."

This is the verse many scholars point to, myself included (formerly), to say this has to be speaking of Rome. They say Rome is the city that sits on seven hills. Well it does, but that isn't what the verse says. It says the woman sits on seven mountains - not hills. Rome does not sit on seven mountains. The question we need to ask here is, "would the Greek word for mountains that is used in this verse, be used for hills if hills were really meant?" We have a precedent in Luke 3.5 where we find the word mountain and the word hill both used in the same sentence. It reads, "Every valley shall be filled and every mountain and hill brought low..."

The Greek word for "mountain" here is "oros" just like in Revelation 17.9, but the Greek word for "hill" is "bounos."

This lets us know that the word "hill" was not the intended word in Rev. 17.9 and it is an important clue that rules Rome out of the picture here.

The seven mountains in verse 9 are representing seven notable kingdoms of the past and the future. This isn't the first time that a mountain has been used to represent a great kingdom. Jeremiah 51.24-25 gives us an example. In verse 24 it is speaking of Babylon and in verse 25 the Lord goes on to say, "Behold I am against you O destroying mountain." Another example is Daniel 2.35 where it says, "...And the stone that struck the image became a great mountain and filled the whole earth." The kingdom that it is speaking of here is the Kingdom of our Lord Jesus Christ.

In Rev. 17.10 we see these seven mountains are also linked to seven kings and in John's time five had fallen, one was, and one was to come. Those seven mountain kingdoms are Egypt, Assyria, Babylon, Medo-Persia, Greece, Rome, and revived Rome. Six of those seven have now fallen and we are living in the revival of what is to be the seventh. So what does it mean for the woman to be sitting on the seven mountain kingdoms? It means she has a residing influence in the realm of what were those kingdom empires with one present exception and that is about to change.

So looking at these past kingdoms let's transition to how they are known as nations today. The heart of the Egyptian kingdom is today Egypt. The U.S. has a small military presence in Egypt, an embassy in Cairo, and provides it $1.557 billion in foreign aid each year.

The heart of the Assyrian and Babylonian kingdoms is known as the nation of Iraq today. The U.S. has a much smaller presence in Iraq now, an embassy in Baghdad, and provides it $1.68 billion in foreign aid each year.

The heart of the Greecian kingdom is the nation of Greece today. The U.S. has a military base in Crete, Greece, an embassy in Athens and they have received foreign aid through U.S. donations to the IMF. The heart of the Roman kingdom is known today as Italy. The U.S. has a military base there and an embassy in Rome, but I've left the Persian kingdom until now as this is the exception I mentioned earlier. The heart of this kingdom is known as the nation of Iran today. The U.S. only has a virtual embassy there and gives it no foreign aid. But I believe this is about to change where the U.S. will soon be involved in a war with Iran making its presence felt very strongly there. The U.S. will try to bring Iran in line with its policy for the world. And yes, the 7th kingdom - the revival of the Roman kingdom.

The U.S. has embassies in every one of those nations and does extensive trade with them, and also has a military presence in all but Iran. In addition, nearly every country of the world has had to use the American dollar as the world's reserve currency up until now. Truly America has made its presence felt around the world in a way no other country has.

There is another important identifier for America in verse 15. It says, "The waters which you saw, where the harlot sits, are peoples, multitudes, nations and tongues." The angel makes it clear Mystery Babylon is made up of many peoples of many different tongues i.e., immigrants from many different countries. But also, within her borders are nations. This is true of all the Indian races such as the Apache nation, the Navajo nation, and the Sioux nation, and on and on we could list them. Again, this certainly describes America, but it doesn't Rome, the Vatican or Iraq.

Let's observe again the ten horns of the beast. Verse 12 and 13 says, "The ten horns which you saw are ten kings who have not yet received a kingdom, but they receive authority as kings with the beast for one hour. These have one purpose, and they give their power and authority to the beast. (NASV)

These ten horns here represent ten kings who are waiting in the wings to exercise their authority and influence. The words, "...who have not yet received a kingdom...." imply they are expecting to rule at some point in time. In the mean time, they are waiting for something to happen to Mystery Babylon or America because she has been in the way of them being able to reign over their respective world regions. These ten kings have great wealth, capacity and abundance with which they could be of help to America in her judgment but they are reserving it to support the beast with. They don't want America to be in control. They want to be in control.

This verse reveals something to us about timing.

The true nature of the ten kings reveal they are very anti-American. Verse 16 says, "And **the ten horns which you saw, and the beast** these will hate the harlot and will make her desolate..."(NASV).

This shows the antichrist will be involved in America's downfall. It shows America's downfall is ongoing right into the seven year tribulation itself. This means Christians will not be here to see the complete downfall of this country. It means our departure time is sooner than what we may have been expecting.

It needs to be pointed out that chapter 17 is not the first time Babylon the Great is mentioned in Revelation.

Babylon the Great is also mentioned in chapter 14 and verse 8. There it says, "Babylon the Great is fallen, is fallen that great city because she has made all nations drink of the wine of the wrath of her fornication."

Chapters 12, 13 and 14 of Revelation represents the midpoint of the seven year tribulation period. One way we know this is verse 9 when it warns people not to take the mark of the beast that was mentioned in chapter 13, and chapter 13 verse 5 reveals there are only 3 1/2 years to go. The important thing to see is the proclamation - that at this point in time Babylon the Great is declared to have fallen. So what this confirms or tells us is that after being half way through the tribulation it shows America is under occupation by foreign forces.

The next statement made to John, in Revelation 17 and verse 14 takes John ahead to the end of the Great Tribulation time. This reveals to John why the ten horns or kings give all their power and authority to the beast. It reads, "These will make war with the Lamb, and the Lamb will overcome them, for He is Lord of lords and King of kings, and those who are with Him are called, chosen and faithful." So when Jesus comes back, this verse reveals, He will wage war on this ungodly world order and his main focus, **initially**, at His return, will be upon the beast and the ten kings.

Now if you remember from verse 8 it was mentioned that those observing the beast were the unsaved. So where were the saints? Here we have the answer to that in the last half of this verse 14, which says, "and those who are with Him are called, chosen and faithful." The saints are already found to be with the King of kings **as He returns** to wage war on the ungodly system.

There is a phrase in Rev. 17.16 - one word actually - that I find very interesting. The phrase is, "...these will hate the harlot, make her desolate..." and "make" is the word of interest. In the Greek it signifies a counter action implying to "avenge" i.e. for something America caused to happen, to them, and they want revenge.

What is happening in the world right now that is causing international turmoil? The one thing that stands out, at the moment, is an on-going currency war. Nations central banks are devaluing currencies so their country's exports will not be curtailed. This allows businesses to maintain jobs and keep people employed but it comes with a terrible side affect; higher and higher inflation and if it progresses long enough nations end up with civil unrest and when it can't be corrected then you have insurrections against governments and blood flows in the streets. That is exactly what is happening under the second seal of the rider on the red horse. America also has a huge bond market bubble which is about to collapse and a lot of foreign nations have purchased those bonds. So when America defaults on her bonds no one gets their investment back and that doesn't sit too well with investors especially foreign countries.

I can think of three nations in particular who have very sizeable bond holdings - China, Japan and Russia. So will these be some of the players among those who get revenge? I think so.

There seems to be a conclusive reason given in verse 18 for excluding Rome as Mystery Babylon. "And the woman whom you saw is that great city which reigns over the kings of the earth." The translators could also have written the words "is to be" for the word "is" as the Greek word "estee" can mean both, "is," or "is to be."

Knowing what we know from identifying Mystery Babylon as America thus far, the words "is to be" makes more sense. So the point the angel was making is the city-state he was referring to **didn't even exit yet** in the world at the time he was speaking to John! In that case, the angel wasn't referring to Rome. Yes, at this point America was indeed a mystery!

It is important to note that **all of the clues** given by the angel must fit to identify the woman not just some of the clues. Only America meets the criteria of all of them!

Chapter Eighteen
The Wine of Her Immorality

The woman in Revelation chapter 17 has been called, "Mystery Babylon the Great" and the Mother of harlots, and I've mentioned in other writings that these names are simply a metonym where she represents the United States. But I want you to notice something else.

Beginning in verse one, the angel says to John, "Come I will show you the judgment of the great harlot who sits on many waters, with whom the kings of the earth committed fornication, and the inhabitants of the earth were made drunk with the wine of her fornication." The language here is full of symbolism.

In particular, we want to understand what is meant by the phrase, "...and the inhabitants of the earth were made drunk with the wine of her fornication." In the Greek, the word "fornication" here means moral depravity and greed. This means being less than honest and unethical to achieve one's aims.

Now let's look at another section of that phrase, "...made drunk with the wine..." People are made to get drunk when they want their senses dulled and then you just might get them to comply with what you want them to do. So the wine then is being used as a bribe. What is it that would make other nations so willing and greedy to get from the U.S.? It is foreign aid and lots of it. This is the wine! Does the scriptures that mention "filthy lucre" come to mind?

I find it interesting that in 1Timothy 3.3 and 3.8 the words "wine" and "filthy lucre" are both used in the same sentence (KJV). But in the more modern translations the word "money" is used for the word "lucre."

With regard to the recipients of this wine, it has many different flavors such as bags of cash, most favored nation trading status, military hardware, millions deposited in secret Swiss bank accounts etc.

So what nation is the most guilty of getting the nations to drink from this cup? Does the United States come to mind?

Chapter Nineteen
The Woman Attracted to Blasphemy

Decoding the symbology of the woman, the harlot, in Revelation 17 is quite revealing. Verse three reads, "So he carried me away in the Spirit into the wilderness. And I saw a woman sitting on a scarlet beast which was full of names of blasphemy, having seven heads and ten horns."

The beast is identified in Rev. 12.3,9 as being the Devil or Satan. In Rev. 17.3 we see the beast also identified with an innate characteristic that attracted the harlot to it. The verse says the beast was full of names of blasphemy. What does the word "blasphemy" mean? It means words that revile God and anything which is religious. This is exactly what we are increasingly seeing in America today! Satanic forces are trying to purge America of anything which pertains to Christianity. They don't even want prayers to end in the name of Jesus.

So in this verse we are actually seeing a spiritual analysis of the woman or America. She is choosing to be allied with Satan's desires for America rather than with God's desires for America. The verse reveals the woman chose to sit on the beast. What does this mean? Sitting on the beast reveals she has chosen the support of the beast and assents to condoning blasphemy.

One way this deceptive change is coming about is through political correctness and the limiting of free speech. This is to prevent anything Christian from offending other people of other faiths or of no faith.

You may not have noticed it, but there is a certain time element associated with this scene of verse three. The first part of this verse states, "So he carried me away in the Spirit into the wilderness."

At this point in time, America is not seen as a land of plenty but as a wilderness. The word "wilderness" really has two aspects to it. First, it conveys being uncultivated and secondly, being uncultured. America hasn't totally succumed yet in this scene but it does show she has been in a precipitous decline. It shows God hasn't been blessing America for quite some time. Scientists have been warning us that the western half of the nation has been drying up for lack of water and is being set up for failed harvests and famine. In fact a lot of farmers in the midwest irrigate only half circle crops as there isn't enough water to irrigate full circles.

Uncultured means our moral and educational values are failing or have failed. Is this true? I believe the answer to that is obvious.

Chapter Twenty
America The Abominable

One of the reasons Revelation chapter 17 has been given to us was to show how abominable America got to be before she was judged! When you continuously fund corruption it grows and spreads like a cancer. We are seeing how corrupt Washington D.C. is - its bureaucracy and the agencies that are under it. But the rot isn't only found there but extends to our liberal institutions as the primary source where the decay process began and flourished. These liberal institutions have brain washed the minds of generations to believe God is irrelevant to the soundness of a society.

One of the first things these institutions did was disavow that God was the creator of this earth and that it came about through evolutionary processes. Accountability to God then gradually went out the window. Then along came the revisionists who rewrote much of our history in that they left out of the historical account references made to God and His providence in the lives of those prominent people who led our country, and the credit they gave to God for the positive outcomes they had experienced. The minds of the people must be dulled you know.

Next the door opened wide for sexual immorality to have free reign in our society. Unmarried people began living together and skipped the marriage vows. So you don't have the stigma for what it is - fornication - it is just called domestic partner living arrangement. What followed was the legalizing of infanticide and roughly 55 million innocent babies have died so far.

It hasn't been enough for America to be diabolical but it is also guilty of funding other nations to do the same such as China. America's diabolical tentacles have been further corrupting the nations. No wonder she was accurately described in Rev. 17.5 as, "The Mother of Harlots and of the Abominations of the Earth." Have you noticed how difficult it is to get justice anymore? This is truly the height of corruption.

It is no wonder then that God says to give Babylon a double judgment in Rev. 18.6-7. "Render to her just as she rendered to you, and repay her double according to her works: in the cup which she mixed, mix double for her. In the measure that she glorified herself and lived luxuriously, in the same measure give her torment and sorrow; for she says in her heart, 'I sit as queen, and am no widow, and will not see sorrow.'"

I certainly have not made an exhaustive list of all of America's sins but I think it is evident they have been national in scope. In the past, God let the cup of iniquity get full before He brought judgment, but it looks to me like America's cup of iniquity is getting very full. God's tolerance for sin does have a limit and He has been sending America wake-up calls, but few seem to be waking up. This is a concern because what follows are wake-up calls that will be much more intense.

Chapter Twenty-One

Identifying America in Isaiah 47

In the past most prophetic teaching has not included references to America because it wasn't recognized in Scripture. You may be thinking that the word America isn't in the Bible, and it isn't in the text as we read it (although, it is in the Bible codes). The Lord has kept this veiled until it was time for America to be understood in prophecy. He kept America hidden through symbolism, and analogy, similar to the way parables are veiled.

Let us look at an example of how descriptive symbolism has been used in Scripture so you can see one way in which America in prophecy will be unveiled. Isaiah 53 verses 3-5 is a passage I believe you will readily recognize. It reads, "He is despised and rejected by men, a Man of sorrows and acquainted with grief. And we hid, as it were, our faces from Him; He was despised and we did not esteem Him. Surely He has borne our grief and carried our sorrows; yet we esteemed Him stricken smitten by God, and afflicted. But He was wounded for our transgressions, He was bruised for our iniquities; the chastisement for our peace was upon Him, and by His stripes we are healed."

It is easy to see, by the <u>descriptive</u> phrases that this is speaking of Jesus, yet Jesus' name is not mentioned here one time. So unique description is one way in which we will discover America in Bible prophecy.

Let us look at one more example in Revelation 11.8. It says, "And their dead bodies will lie in the street of the great city which spiritually is called Sodom and Egypt, where also our Lord was crucified."

Here we see the description actually alludes to the city of Jerusalem, but the name Jerusalem is not mentioned, rather names of places that would not make you think of Jerusalem at all. So how will America be identified in Bible prophecy? Believe it or not, we will identify America in Scripture through the phrase "daughter of Babylon," and through descriptive analogy as we look at Isaiah chapter 47.

I used to think anyone who believed America was Babylon of the end-time was way off in left field until I became open enough (after several years) to study it out for myself.

In reading through Isaiah chapter 47 you notice it seems to be speaking of Babylon and therefore you might assume that this must be historical Babylon. But if you read it carefully you will find **over a half dozen places** that reveal why this can't be referring to the ancient kingdom of Babylon, and this is key to understanding the prophecy.

First of all, it needs to be understood that in both the old and new testament eras when anyone referred to ancient Babylon it was always just as "Babylon," or the **"kingdom of Babylon"** (KJV Daniel 4.29). Speaking of Babylon, in any other way, would allude to an enigma with regard to the prophecy, and that is what we find in Isaiah 47.

In verse one it says, "Come down and sit in the dust, O Virgin daughter of Babylon; Sit on the ground without a throne, O daughter of the Chaldeans for you shall no longer be called tender and delicate."

At first glance it looks like it is speaking of historical Babylon in verse one, only it isn't, and in analyzing this verse we will see why. If you noticed, "daughter of Babylon" is specified here - not just "Babylon." This is our first clue.

The next clue is borne out from the Hebrew with regard to the word "virgin." "Virgin" can also imply "separate." So the phrase can be read as "separate daughter of Babylon." It needs to be seen that the word "daughter" implies a symbolic Babylon that comes later in time. We know Isaiah is not talking about ancient Babylon because of the word virgin which indicates one that is separate.

Notice from verse one that it is specific in speaking of the <u>daughter</u> of the Chaldeans - rather than the Chaldeans of ancient Babylon. Obviously this proposes a similarity between the two Babylons from the words, "...O daughter of the Chaldeans..." Here's why. The Chaldeans were the devoted people of science in the ancient kingdom. They were highly thought of for solving difficult problems. In our modern era many nations have their scientists and engineers, but among all countries of the world <u>what country is best known for its know-how</u>? Without question, the whole world knows America is renown for its know-how!

Students from all over the world want to come to America's universities to be educated. Russia and Red China are great countries too, but American know-how has helped make them more so than they otherwise would be today. For example, when Nixon was president he made it possible for the Soviet Union to get what ever they wanted from our patent office, and when Clinton was in office he did the same for Red China. It is no secret that the Japanese have copied our technology extensively among the more notable countries that have been helped by it.

World class know-how is such an important point in identifying America here that it is mentioned even more clearly in verse ten.

Verse 10 says, "...You have said, 'No one sees me;" Your wisdom and your knowledge have warped you; and you have said in your heart, 'I am, and there is no one else besides me.'"

The words "no one sees me" has strong overtones that the daughter of Babylon has stealth technology. If it is meant to be understood this way, then this would be a general "timing indicator" for when judgment will come upon her in the latter days. In other words, the ensuing period of judgment wouldn't come upon her before she had stealth technology, but now she has it.

The words, "you have said in your heart, 'I am, and there is no one else beside me'" reveals the city-state we are analyzing believes it has a technological edge over all others. This is definitely true of America, but it is not true of Iraq or Iraq's Babylon or of Rome in our end-time generation that a few have proposed as being Mystery Babylon. They do not have a technological edge over all other nations which disqualifies them as being the daughter of Babylon. So we know this prophecy is not referring to the nations of Italy or Iraq, but it does fit America better than any other nation we might consider as a likely candidate.

If we look again at verse one we will see it is a general overview of the chapter in terms of the chastisement determined to come upon this country, and it tells us quite a lot. For example, the word for "Come down" in the Hebrew, is "yarad" and has the connotation to bring down or to be forcibly subdued. The words "sit in the dust" reveal two things. First, the word "sit" has the connotation, in the Hebrew, to endure. In other words, **this chastisement is for a period of time** that will not end quickly.

The word "dust" in the Hebrew also has the connotation of ashes and rubbish. So the Lord has revealed to us in just those few words that this country will be attacked and occupied for a period of time.

The next words of verse one, "sit on the ground **without a throne**" reveal the present government will be done away with. The word "throne" in the Hebrew has the connotation of covered or protected seat of authority. This means the seat of government itself, and the agencies that protect it, will be done away with by the forces that will subdue this country.

The way I understand this chapter it seems the chastisement starts off slowly and then as time goes by the pace of it dramatically increases. I believe there are two main phases to this chastisement. There is a decline phase followed by a judgment phase. There will be a brief pause where the Lord will look for signs of repentance before He allows the judgment phase to begin. I believe we are already in the decline phase now and that it began a few months before the devastation of the World Trade Center buildings. From verse one and verse five it appears that the first two things that become evident in this chastisement of America are (1) an economic downturn and (2) what could be viewed as terrorist attacks. We read in verse one, "...for you shall no longer be called tender and delicate." This implies much of this country has known an easygoing life style in the past, but this easy life style will begin to diminish. If there is one thing that can make this change for the worse it is a national economic downturn that is now being perpetuated at the Federal level. As you know, recession, deflation, and inflation can be typical factors in an economic downturn. It is implied in this verse that something will compound and prolong this downturn.

70

Evidence that this country is in an economic downturn is to look at states revenues. Many have lost so much revenue that they claim to be billions of dollars in debt. Does the fact that tens of thousand of companies having left the United States to re-establish themselves overseas have anything to do with this? Large coporations have under funded pension plans to the tune of billions of dollars. Obviously these companies earnings have been affected in their ability to compete in the market place.

Millions who took out second mortgages on their homes spent the money or made poor investments with it are now burdened with the debt. Personal bankruptcies are at an all time high and the Federal Reserve has introduced factors that worsen the downturn. It has allowed the printing presses to run to cover deficit spending by the government. This causes our currency to be devalued decreasing its purchasing power. Foreign oil exporters now require more of our dollars to purchase their oil because of the devalued dollar. What about the higher prices at the gas pump or increased shipping costs?

Another factor which is compounding the downturn is the increase of inflation caused by huge **off budget** items in the Federal government which some economists say is now approaching one trillion dollars for just one year. For example, billions of dollars were spent to fund the Iraq and Afghanistan war and its reconstruction, and the new prescription drug coverage for Medicare etc. How does this cause inflation? The Federal government must sell bonds and securities to raise the funds for these off budget expenditures. In order to entice buyers for such large outlays the government must raise the yield on the bonds they sell. since long term interest rates are tied to the yield on these bonds it causes rates to go up.

These higher rates are passed on to home mortgages, corporate borrowing, and credit card rates etc. When home mortgages rates go up people don't buy nearly as many new homes and this causes a downturn in the real estate market. When corporations curtail getting loans their companies don't expand and don't remain competitive. When credit card rates go up people cut way back on their use of these cards and retail stores see less business. The result is an economic contraction.

Verse two and the first part of verse three reveal this country is invaded and occupied after the economy has been in a severe downturn. It says, "Take the millstones and grind meal. Remove the veil, take off the skirt, uncover the thigh, pass through the rivers. Your nakedness shall be uncovered, yes your shame will be seen."

Take the words, "Take the millstones and grind meal" is the same as saying the time for conveniences and luxury is over. Prepare to do your work the hard way. It will be like turning the clock back 50 years or so. The conveniences we expect will decline. This country's problems will get worse because of war. The country will be invaded and occupied. One way we know this is because of the words "Your nakedness shall be uncovered." The word "uncovered" in the Hebrew has the additional connotation of being taken captive.

We must remember that this country is trying to portray itself to the world (according to the context of this chapter) as a virgin (meaning morally justified in her role in the world), as the daughter of science (daughter of the Chaldeans), and as the Lady of kingdoms. But the Lord is saying, but "your nakedness shall be uncovered." "Your nakedness" implies what this country doesn't want the world to see or know about it.

America doesn't want the world to know and believe that its fall from grace was the result of it trading its commitment to God for becoming lovers of pleasures rather than lovers of God. The words, "yes your shame will be seen" imply its disgrace. This country will not show its shame until it has been disgraced. What would disgrace America? Would it not be loss of power, loss of a vibrant economy, loss of its Constitutional freedoms, and loss of freedom of religion?

Jesus addresses a situation that parallels this one in Revelation 3.17-18 saying, "Because you say, I am rich, have become wealthy, and have need of nothing - and do not know that you are wretched, miserable, poor, blind, and naked. I counsel you to buy from Me gold refined in the fire, that you may be rich; and white garments, that you may be clothed, that the shame of your nakedness may not be revealed; and anoint your eyes that you may see."

We return to the last words of verse two that say, "pass through the rivers." They are full of symbolism. But in the Hebrew here, the word "rivers" is really referring to the invading forces or armies. The word "rivers" in the Hebrew is "nehar" and comes from the root word which means to assemble to flow together - like different streams coming together to form a river. This represents, and thus reveals, a converging of forces for a common cause. The words "pass through" come from the Hebrew word "abar" and can have the additional connotation to be carried away by. So what this is saying is that a sizeable number of people will be forcibly displaced to locations more favorable to the occupation forces. FEMA type camps come to mind. Do you think occupation forces will make use of these camps so conveniently available to them?

The Lord is allowing this judgment to unfold in this way because He is angry with a people that have rebelled against Him while at the same time claiming to be a Christian nation. He will no longer allow for the hypocrisy and the evil that He sees. So we see the last part of verse three saying, "I will take vengeance, and I will not arbitrate with a man." The time to arbitrate with God is right now and it is done through repentance, submitting to the Lordship of Jesus Christ and establishing a daily relationship with Him. If this is your life style then you are in His safekeeping. If not then you have cause to worry.

Now going on to verse four we have <u>additional evidence</u> that this is not speaking about ancient or rebuilt Babylon. It says, "As for our Redeemer, the Lord of hosts is His Name, The Holy One of Israel."

This verse indicates that the people of this country have based their religion on the one known as the Redeemer, The Holy One of Israel. The word "Redeemer" here is the same as that used in the book of Job 19.25 where Job said, "For I know that my Redeemer lives, and He shall stand at last on the earth."

Only one has come to earth as the Redeemer of mankind and He is Jesus Christ. This prophecy is speaking about a time in which Jesus Christ is known and has been proclaimed to the world. This would not apply to historic Babylon, but it does speak of America because it was **founded** upon the Judeo-Christian religion. Ancient Babylon did not embrace Jesus Christ nor was He known to them.

The next calamity Isaiah mentions in verse 5 is also <u>another identifier</u> for America where it says, "Sit in silence, and go into darkness, O daughter of the Chaldeans; For you shall no longer be called The Lady of Kingdoms."

Daughter of the Chaldeans is being addressed here, which alludes to the scientific technologies, in particular, that drives this country's economy. America has been known as the leading industrialized nation and for its high tech manufacturing abilities. Other countries could fit this description to a point, but only one is the "daughter of the Chaldeans" the one known for its know-how. But in this verse we see the words "sit in silence and go into darkness."

This implies electrical grid problems. Manufacturing plants are very quiet when all the noisy machinery inside comes to a standstill. The lights go out leaving you to sit in the darkness. I know since I have experienced it first hand. There are several things that could bring down the electrical grid and it could be a combination of things, but what we do know is that the scripture has foretold to us that it will happen.

Once the electrical grid goes down it could possibly bring most of the country to a standstill. Think about it. How many businesses use computerized sales machines for reading bar codes? How about the literally billions of dollars that are sent by wire between banks as well as overseas transactions every day? You don't pump fuel at gas stations when there isn't any electricity. Travel becomes very restricted. Refrigerators in homes quit working and in time food begins to spoil. Most homes would not have any hot water or lights or air conditioning. No traffic lights would cause serious traffic snarls creating a great deal of frustration and delays. When the north-eastern states had their blackout that affected 50 million people, and the UK and Italy had theirs all within about a week of each other was that just coincidence? Doesn't that show how vulnerable electrical grid systems are?

Verse five also describes this country as "Lady of Kingdoms." "Lady" in the Hebrew means mistress, and mistress means one who has limited authority, power and control over others. As far as control goes, America has been criticized for trying to be the world's policeman, and many foreign nations despise her in that role. She strives to have a controlling interest in other countries affairs in a variety of ways such as through most favored nation trade status, and seeing other countries' currencies tied to the value of its dollar. She is called "Lady" here, which would allude to her skills in diplomacy. America is also a leading country in providing foreign aid giving her a very controlling influence in other countries affairs.

This just simply provides further confirmation concerning this Babylon's identity of the end-time. Even though Iraq has been an important source of oil energy it has certainly not been known as the Lady of kingdoms in our present day. Modern day Rome, though she has had considerable influence many centuries ago, is definitely not the mistress of kingdoms today. Neither can she say, "I am, and there is no one else beside me," in the sense of economic, technological, or military supremacy.

Some might think verse five could also apply to the Vatican. It has a lot of influence in nations that are predominately Catholic, I agree, but not a lot in Islamic countries or China, Russia, Japan North Korea etc. Neither is it known as the country of world renowned know-how. It just doesn't meet all the necessary criteria given for identifying this Babylon here. All that identifying criteria was given by the Lord for a reason - **so we wouldn't miss identifying correctly** this end-time Babylon as it is mentioned here.

Now we come to verse six. It says, "I was angry with My people; I have profaned My inheritance, and given them into your hand. You showed them no mercy; on the elderly you laid your yoke very heavily."

The words, "I was angry with My people" refers to the Lord being angry with those who consider themselves Christians but are in no way living like Christians. We know this because verse four, which we looked at earlier, pointed to the Redeemer as Lord of this people. The words "I have profaned My inheritance" means, for the purpose of this chastisement the Lord will now view and treat His people who call themselves Christians but haven't had a born again experience and therefore no real relationship with Him as being secular. The words "and given them into your hand" imply giving them into the hands of an anti-Christian element. The words "you showed them no mercy" reveal a severe backlash of persecution against them. Yes, religious persecution breaks out and it will get to be very intense. The words "on the elderly you laid your yoke very heavily" is referring to an imposition laid upon its senior citizens by its own government. It isn't clear what this is, but one thing that would sure do it would be a collapse of the social security system or an intentional devaluation of the dollar causing high inflation for people on a fixed income.

Millions of the elderly rely upon their social security monthly checks. Many of these checks are for people with medical retirements because they can no longer work. When large cities go bankrupt it even affects government pensions. If the elderly are faced with the need to look for jobs again so they can survive it would be a heavy yoke indeed.

The secrets these scriptures are revealing to us are any-thing but what we want to hear. But isn't it true that people in general will not change and turn back to God unless pressure is put upon them to do so? This is confirmed in verse seven where it says, "you did not take these things to heart." That is another way of saying that you did not take these things seriously.

In verse seven it reveals **the general time period** of the daughter of Babylon we are analyzing. It says, "And you said, 'I shall be a lady forever.' So that you did not take these things to heart, nor remember the latter end of them."

Those words "latter end" in the Hebrew mean future end, or as so often stated, the end-time. So this daughter of Babylon, of the time of the end, is specified here - not historical Babylon. As though we didn't have enough information already to make a positive ID verse 8a goes on to say, "Therefore here this now, you who are given to pleasures, who dwell securely, who say in your heart, 'I am, and there is no one else beside me...'"

The words "given to" in the Hebrew has wide application of meanings as: pay for, charge for, perform for, yield to and be occupied with. The word "pleasures" here refers to all types of sensual gratification. This verse is not describing some sinful sexual pleasure, but pleasures in the general sense. For example, being wined and dined in fine restaurants, pursuing the luxuries of life, Disney type fun parks, casinos, golfing, bingo night, yachting, surfing, bungee jumping, boat racing, auto racing, ocean cruises, boxing events, football events, baseball games, basket ball games, video games, movie theaters, TV, horse races, dog races, concerts, plays fishing trips, skiing, snowboarding, mountain climbing, safaris, county fairs, circuses, dancing, rollerblading, etc. meet the general criteria for pleasures.

It isn't that the Lord is condemning all types of pleasures here, but merely to point out that this Babylon, in particular, is **occupied** with them providing yet another way we can identiy who He is speaking about. Is there any other country more given to pleasures than America that also meets all the other aforementioned criteria to identify her? I don't know of any. Another identifier is in verse 8 that says, "who dwell securely."

Americans haven't built walls around their cities. America has been a super power both militarily and economically and its Constitiution has provided, up to now, important liberties that other nations are envious to have. This verse certainly does not apply to the Iraqis striving to have the necessities of life. Neither does this verse apply to Rome, Italy, nor the Vatican because they are not super powers as specified in this verse. The Vatican is certainly not given to pleasures.

Verses 8b and 9a go on to pinpoint <u>the uniqueness</u> of this judgment upon the daughter of Babylon. It reads, "I shall not sit as a widow, nor shall I know the loss of children; but these two things shall come to you in a moment, in one day: the loss of children and widowhood. They shall come upon you in their fullness."

This verse is describing a very quick and dramatic reduction in the population in the words, "in a moment in one day." The word "moment" in the Hebrew means in an instant. The Medes and Persians didn't destroy Babylon. That didn't happen until many years later under Xerxes and the Parthians. This is another reason we know it isn't speaking about ancient Babylon here. Only in the 20th and 21st century is it possible to bring about massive destruction, in an instant, with nuclear warheads. <u>This specifically underscores an end-time judgment.</u>

The Lord gives another reason for the coming judgments. Verse 9b and 10a says,"Because of the multitude of your sorceries, for the great abundance of your enchantments. For you have trusted in your wickedness."

The Lord is saying because you have turned away from Me I allow these judgment events to come. "Sorceries" in the Hebrew means witchcraft. Is there an upsurge in witchcraft today? What about some of the movies coming out of Hollywood? Witchcraft means simply magic that deceives. But a great many people in America have left themselves open to deception of all kinds. Deception is to believe a lie.

One of the biggest lies in the history of the world is trying to make the world believe that macro evolution occurred denying God as Creator of all things. This has given rise to Humanism, Fascism, Communism etc. They all have one thing in common. The denial of any accountability to God. This is the lie! This has opened the door to atrocities that are exercised even today in abortions, and this is wickedness, and it happens in America! Furthermore, Americans "trust in this wickedness" **because it has been legalized** from the highest court of the land.

In verses 12 and 13 God includes enchanters (those who cast spells), and astrologers, and monthly prognosticators. In other words, those who seek demonic insight for guidance. You can find it it horoscopes in almost every newspaper, from psychics, fortune-tellers, and other related sources in America. God specifically warned His people not to seek out this kind of advice that wasn't from Him, but it is freely done in America.

We can say without any reservation that all of these identifiers of the end-time daughter of Babylon apply to America - not just some of them.

The Lord is quite specific about a particular aspect of this judgment starting in verse 11. He says, "Therefore evil will come upon you; You shall not know from where it arises. And trouble shall fall upon you; You will not be able to put it off. And desolation shall come upon you suddenly, which you shall not know.

The word "evil" in the Hebrew here means an exceedingly great calamity that leaves sorrow and trouble. The words "you shall not know from where it arises," means it comes upon you in a way you didn't expect it. The words "you shall not be able to put it off" means there will be no way to cancel the coming calamity because it happens suddenly and it results in desolation. The words "which you shall not know" is like saying, "he didn't know what hit him."

One more thing you need to see in this verse is that it says this evil or calamity arises (to rise up), and then falls to bring about great destruction. In our modern day vernacular, this verse could be indicating America's enemies will launch intercontinental ballistic missiles from submarines at close range so as to cut short any response time needed to intercept them ("You will not be able to put it off"), and it will also deny precious warning time needed for people to escape these targeted cities. Ah, you say, but this will never happen because America has an underwater sensor system to detect where enemy submarines are at all time. This is only partly true. It was deactivated under the Clinton administration. I have been unable to find out if it was ever reactivated.

Now verse 14 describes the scene of destruction in a little more detail saying, "Behold, they shall be as stubble, the fire shall burn them; they shall not deliver themselves from the power of the flame; It shall not be a coal to be warmed by, nor a fire to sit before!

The word "burn" here in the Hebrew means to be set on fire and be completely consumed by it. The word "flame" in the Hebrew here means a bright flash from the head of. In this case we understand it to be from the warheads of missiles. We would have to agree that this is no ordinary fire. It would have been totally foreign to the ancients. The Hebrew word for "flame" here can mean direction of, ordinance and terror of. This lends some support to these being guided missiles, and it definitely is the kind of flame that evokes terror.

Now we come to verse 15. It says, "Thus shall they be to you with whom you have labored, your merchants from your youth; They shall wander each one to his quarter. No one shall save you."

This verse reveals what appears to be an almost total collapse in the economy at this point. The merchants, or trading partners, depart from us. This has quite strong implications that imports and exports cease, at least for the duration of this judgment. It seems to imply most outside trading is curtailed. The whole world will be affected by America's fall only they don't see the implications of this until it is too late.

The last part of verse 15 is the saddest of all. It says, "No one shall save you." This means America's so called friends in NATO will not come to her aid. America will be abandoned - left to go it alone.

Chapter Twenty-Two
America Contended Against God

In a previous commentary titled "America The Abominable" I gave several examples of her abominations but I also left out a very serious one. In Rev. 17.6 John is shocked when he sees it. "I saw the woman drunk with the blood of the saints and with the blood of the martyrs of Jesus..." You may be thinking as I did - martyrs in America? Well sadly to say, we have confirmation of that in Rev. 19.2. "For true and righteous are His judgments, because He has judged the great harlot who corrupted the earth with her fornication; and He has avenged on her the blood of His servants shed by her."

It appears that what seals America's doom is allowing and sanctioning the killing of the saints. No other atrocious activity is mentioned after this in Rev. 17. America is at war.

We go to Jeremiah 50.22-24 and see America, the policeman of the world (the hammer), being addressed. "A sound of battle is in the land and of great destruction. How the hammer of the whole earth has been cut apart and broken! How Babylon has become a desolation among the nations! I have laid a snare for you: you have indeed been trapped, O Babylon, and you were not aware; you have been found and also caught because you have contended against the Lord." The word "caught" means captured in the Hebrew. This reveals America will come under occupation.

Now verse 28 confirms that we are not talking about Babylon under Belshazzar. "The voice of those who flee and escape from the land of Babylon declares in Zion the vengeance of the Lord our God, the vengeance of His temple."

First of all, when the Jews left Babylon under Cyrus they weren't fleeing or escaping. They were free to go. What we are actually seeing in this verse are Jews fleeing America because of the war and going to Zion or Israel, and declaring there, that this is God's judgment on America for the killing of His saints. Yes, the saints represent His temple (1Cor.6.19; Eph.2.21).

Now there is more information in Scripture on how America is being destroyed than what has been mentioned previously. Jeremiah 51.1 says, "Thus says the Lord: Behold I will raise up against Babylon, against those who dwell in the midst of those who rise up against Me a destroying wind." In verse 2 what follows is the invasion of the land from all sides. From this passage I believe what precedes the invasion of forces is a nuclear strike where each nuclear blast destroys with a 600 mph wind. I believe we have further confirmation of this in Isaiah 47. Verse one directs our attention to the daughter of Babylon.

The daughter of Babyon means it isn't the Babylon of Belshazzars day but a Babylon that comes later in time. We have previously identified that this end-time Babylon is America so we know Isaiah 47 is referring to America. So let's go to verse 11 where we are told how desolation comes to America. "Therefore evil shall come upon you; You shall not know from where it <u>arises</u> and trouble shall <u>fall</u> upon you; you will not be able to put it off. And desolation shall come upon you suddenly..."

What rises and falls and brings catastrophic destruction? My answer would be exploding of nuclear tipped missiles. I'm even more convinced of this when the verse says it happens "suddenly."

In Rev.18 it mentions three times that this destruction takes place in the span of one hour (v.10, 17 & 19). When I served aboard a fleet ballistic missile submarine we had the capability to launch all 16 missiles in under an hour.

Governments know nuclear tipped missiles aren't cheap and they take a long time to produce so if they are going to use them they will use them where they can do the most damage. Those targets will be large metropolitan areas and military bases. Secondly, some places will not be targeted by these weapons so the infrastructure won't be destroyed making it easier for the invasion force to invade. The enemy will probably want to keep the oil refineries intack because they are a highly valued prize they will want to take over.

If we are agreed that the scripture is speaking about America being attacked with nuclear weapons then we can also get a good idea of who our attackers are because there aren't very many countries that have these weapons and this capability. It looks like Russia and Red China will be at least two of the big aggressive nations involved here. So if a person is living at least 20 miles away from a target zone they stand a very good chance of not being harmed by a nuclear blast.

There is a bit of an enigma in Rev. 17.6 about who these saints are whose blood has been shed in America. One might believe these saints were killed before the rapture took place. What we don't know is how long before the antichrist is revealed that the rapture takes place. What we do know is that sometime before America has fallen (i.e. where she can no longer defend herself) the rapture takes place. We also know that some time during this war God calls His people to come out of America (Rev.18.4). "And I heard another voice <u>from heaven</u> saying, Come out of her My people, lest you share in her sins and lest you receive of her plagues." So it is possible to escape these troubles if one hears the call. How many are listening for it today?

Chapter Twenty-Three
America's Double Judgment

As you know it was in Revelation chapter 17 that we were able to identify mystery Babylon as the United States. But this Babylon is mentioned in chapters 14, 16, 17, 18, and 19 and in every case it is the same Babylon being referenced. It was in chapter 18 that we were informed America would undergo a double judgment. It is in chapter 16 verses 17-19 that reveals America's second judgment takes place under the 7th bowl judgment. But what we are really curious about is the first judgment.

How will people recognize that they are in a judgment from God? At first, people will choose to be in denial with regard to a catastrophic occurrence. You'll hear them say, "Oh, that has happened before - 30 years ago. We just need to band together and help each other out." The defining change is the frequency and the severity of such occurrences to get them to realize this is way beyond the norm.

Sometimes observing an unsettling trend will get people's attention. For example, consider the following states: AK, AR, CT, DE, DC, HI, ID, IA, KS ME, MS, MT, NE, NV, NH, NM, ND, OK, OR, RI, SD, UT, VT, WV, and WY. The combined population of all these states is how many people in this country that are now on food stamps. Does this represent a blessing or a curse on this country? The true unemployment in this country is very high and all efforts to lower it seem to fail. Violence is increasing in the big cities and the schools. Cities are starting to declare bankruptcy, and many businesses are shutting down. Looks like God has withdrawn His blessing on this country.

These downtrends are hinting at a greater coming judgment. America's first judgment will become very severe for the country. Many voices have warned the people already. But instead of heeding these warnings I have seen increased rebellion and hatred against God. What usually comes next is God allows plagues to come. What do I base this on? Do you remember Moses' encounter with the Pharoah of Egypt? That is exactly what happened to Egypt when Pharoah dismissed the warnings.

A plague can be rather daunting because it is usually an event that man has very little ability to control such as severe long term weather conditions. We know that a prolonged lack of rain causes famine conditions and this is one of the plagues that will be part of America's judgment. We saw this in Rev. 17.3 where John observed the woman in the wilderness. At some point one starts to hear words such as, "this is a God forsaken country." People also become more aware that they are in a judgment from God when their problems are the result of compounding events where several are happening at once.

The U.S.A. is about to enter that phase. The government continues to let its currency be devalued causing inflation creep. Our government is doing absolutely nothing to stop this downward trend and if not stopped it leads to a collapsed currency. Yes, the events are already starting to compound. We are already seeing sequential catastrophic events in tornadoes and hurricanes which is taxing insurance companies to compensate those losses. At what point do these funds dry up? Tornadoes and hurricanes aren't even mentioned in Scripture with regard to judging America but something even more devastating is - earthquakes, and war. Are these storm clouds present and real or just imagined?

Chapter Twenty-Four
America's First Judgment

In my previous commentaries I've mentioned what some of America's troubles are and how they are getting progressively worse with time. But the most feared plague to come upon America will be war. In Rev. 17.16 it speaks of this war but not in much detail. It is more clearly understood in passages in Jeremiah 50 and 51, but at the same time it is not straight forward. What I mean by that is, it is like someone who has done a computer search for information on say the city of Springfield. What pops up is information on Springfield MO, and Springfield OR but it is left up to you to sort out which is which.

We determine by the context whether it is the Babylon of Jeremiah's time or the end-time Babylon of America, and sometimes the context applies to both. Also if you run across a reference to "daughter of Babylon" that refers to America as well. I am not going to give a full analysis of both chapters as it would be too lengthy but I will begin by selecting verses 14-16 of chapter 50.

Verse 14 says, "Put yourselves in array against Babylon all around..." This indicates that when America is attacked she will be invaded from the north, east, south and west. "...All you who bend the bow, shoot at her, <u>spare no arrows</u> for she has sinned against the Lord." Notice the first thing the enemy deploys is airborne missiles.

Verse 15 says, "Shout against her all around; she has given her hand..." This means America has exhausted her defense capabilities and has nothing left to give. This would also tell me that America's ammunition stock piles had been depleted somewhat before this invasion occurred.

"...Her foundations have fallen..." This refers to the underpinnings of the Constitution. The people are demoralized. Their liberties were trampled underfoot by its own government. "...Her walls are thrown down for it is the vengeance of the Lord. Take vengeance on her." The word "walls" here mean to join which refers to the 50 states as having been united but at this point in time each is so distressed they can't come to each other's aid. They are each on their own.

Verse 16 says, "Cut off the sower from Babylon and him who handles the sickle at harvest time..." This shows two things that the war is prolonged for a period of time and that planting and harvesting of the crops isn't being done probably because of the raging conflict. To say nothing of the drought conditions the war compounds the famine conditions. At this point, having food will be nearly priceless. "...For fear of the oppressing sword everyone shall turn to his own people, and everyone shall flee to his own land." This reveals a country that was comprised of immigrants that now see their prior homeland as a more favorable place to be because of the war here.

One more verse I want to quote in this commentary is verse 46. "At the noise of the taking of Babylon the earth trembles and the cry is heard among the nations." This reveals America is no longer able to defend herself and comes under occupation. All foreign aid is cut off - no more charity to the nations. The nations of the world realize this super power is no longer such. America had represented freedom, hope and trade to the world but no longer.

Chapter Twenty-Five
The Feast of Trumpets

The last book of the Bible - The Revelation of Jesus Christ is crucial to bring closure to the canon of Scripture. It could also have had a subtitle such as: revealing old testament prophecies for the end-time. I've sometimes wondered if Israel understood that the feasts and ordinances which they kept under the leadership of Moses would receive a final fulfillment at some point in time.

The Passover was fulfilled by Jesus at Calvary for example. The Feast of Weeks was fulfilled at Pentecost. That 50 day period was first initiated when Israel came out of Egypt after the Passover until the giving of the law at Mt. Sinai. This is why the disciples were instructed to wait in the upper room at Jerusalem because the new covenant which Jesus declared (Matt. 26.28) was made official on the day of Pentecost to include both Jew and Gentile and that is the official designation of the birth of the Church. Yes, that was the fulfillment of the Feast of Weeks.

The Feast of Firstfruits will be fulfilled at the rapture of the Church and the Feast of Ingathering will be fulfilled with the resurrection and translation of the great tribulation saints as they are the last of the harvest of those who will participate in reigning with Christ in the Kingdom of God as I've mentioned previously in another commentary. But what about the Feast of Trumpets? This festival was actually celebrated before the Feast of Ingathering.

There are three primary things we know about the Feast of Trumpets from Leviticus 23.24. First, it convened a holy convocation. Second, it invoked rest from one's labors, and third it was to be a memorial of what God had done for you, and was to be a time of praise.

Now the question is - where in the book of Revelation do we find this criteria met? Answer - the first part of chapter 19. Prior to chapter 19, the world will have been in great turmoil trying to eradicate all vestiges of Christianity, and God has been paying back His enemies through the trumpet and bowl judgments, and now we are nearing the end of the great tribulation.

The first thing we see in chapter 19 is a holy convocation (i.e. the great assembly of God's people). Verse 1 says, "...I heard a loud voice of a great multitude in heaven..." The next thing they do is declare their memorial, a reflection on what God did for them (v.2). "For true and righteous are His judgments because He has judged the great harlot who corrupted the earth with her fornication and He has avenged on her the blood of His servants shed by her."

This memorial is intended to invoke praise to God. This praise to God is mentioned five separate times in verses 1-6, and will be the most profound time of praise to God up to this point as depicted in verse six. It says, "And I heard as it were, the voice of a great multitude, as the sound of many waters, and the sound of mighty thunderings, saying Alleluia! For the Lord God omnipotent reigns!" The last of the criteria is simply understood - rest from their labors. The apostle Paul stated it this way in 2Thess. 1.6-7. "...It is a righteous thing with God to repay with tribulation those who trouble you, and to give you who are troubled **rest** with us when the Lord Jesus is revealed from heaven..."

The Feast of Trumpets is a time of blowing the trumpets. This is a grand prelude to what immediately follows in chapter 19; the marriage of the Lamb (v.7). This is what the fulfillment of the Feast of Trumpets is all about.

92

Chapter Twenty-Six
Misplacing The New Jerusalem

At some point in the past you may have heard it taught that the New Jerusalem will come down from heaven upon this earth during the 1,000 year reign of Christ. There are a couple of problems with this and its huge size applies to both of them. Rev. 21.16 says, "The city is laid out as a square; its length is as great as its breadth. And he measured the city with the reed: twelve thousand furlongs. Its length, breadth, and height are equal." Depending upon which translation you have 12,000 furlongs is equal to either 1400 miles or 1500 miles long.

So if you set down on the earth a city that is 1500 miles long on each side that equals 2,250,000 square miles of city. The question is, where would you put it? The entire nation of Israel is only 7,849 square miles in size. If you set it down on any of the inhabitable land area you would wipe out a number of nations in the process. Obviously something is wrong with this picture here.

But then there is a second problem. Say you did find a place to put it; you wouldn't be able to get into it. Why not? Because of the curvature of the earth. To exaggerate a little to make my point it would sit like trying to balance a book on a ball. The sides of the city would extend over the curvature of the land by 70 miles on all sides, and I don't know of anyone who can jump that far to get into one of the city gates. Well, what if the city were only 1400 miles on a side then you would only have to jump 60 miles to get in.

The point is, this earth just simply isn't big enough for a city of that size.

The answer to this dilemna is found in Rev. 21.1. Verse one establishes the basis for the context we have been considering. "Now I saw a new heaven and a new earth for the first heaven and first earth had passed away..." So what John was actually seeing was a New Jerusalem coming down upon an entirely new earth. This tells us something about the new earth. It will be big enough to accomodate this huge city so that people will be able to get in the city gates. Therefore, the new earth will be considerably larger than our present earth.

Sometimes what isn't said provides additional information as well. With regard to this new earth you don't hear God saying that He will take one of the planets He has already made to be the new earth. No, rather He says in Isaiah 65.17, "For behold, I create new heavens and a new earth..." The words imply it hasn't been done yet. This will be an entirely new creation from what we can now see in the heavens with our telescopes.

We have not seen God perform a mighty act of creation like that before. Maybe He is going to put on a show for us.

Chapter Twenty-Seven
The Desolation of Jerusalem

The prophetic events Jesus spoke of in Matthew 24, Mark 13, and Luke 21 are all very similar. One particular difference found in Luke's account provides some additional information about the desolation of Jerusalem. I'm referring to the passage in Luke 21.20-24. There is this belief that since Israel has become an independent nation state again she will never again be uprooted. It will come as a surprise to some that this is not completely true.

In Luke 21.20-21 Jesus states that when the time comes that Jerusalem is being surrounded by armies that those in the city and Judea need to flee to the mountains. Jesus is being very specific about the time this occurs in verse 22. "For these are the days of vengeance, that <u>all</u> <u>things</u> which are written may be fulfilled." Even though there are some similarities to the destruction of Jerusalem in 70 A.D. this is not what Jesus is alluding to here. Jesus is speaking about the 1948 end-time generation because He is saying that all the things written about the days of vengeance against Israel will be fulfilled when these events are completed.

Jesus is describing what the final days and perhaps weeks of aggression against Jerusalem will be like. Jesus indicates in verse 24 that those in Jerusalem "...will fall by the edge of the sword and be led away captive into all nations." But there is a silver lining around this dark cloud. First of all, only half of the city is subjected to captivity, and secondly, this dispersion of Jews will be of a very short duration.

Zechariah 14.2 clarifies. "For I will gather all the nations to battle against Jerusalem; the city shall be taken, the houses rifled, and the women ravished. Half of the city shall go into captivity, but the remnant of the people shall not be cut off from the city."

To give you an idea of how severe the war of nations goes against Israel before Jesus intervenes Zechariah 13.8 says, "And it shall come to pass in all the land, says the Lord, that two-thirds in it shall be cut off and die, but one-third shall be left in it."

Matthew's account addresses the problems at the beginning of Jacob's trouble with the antichrist coming into the temple and setting up the abomination of desolation that forces the religious Jews to flee the city where Luke's account addresses the events at the end of Jacob's trouble.

You see only the antichrist's army - just one army - when he comes into Jerusalem to stop the sacrifices. This is revealed in Daniel 8.12. "Because of transgression an army was given over to the horn to oppose the daily sacrifices..." But Jesus differentiates the time period in Luke 21.20 when He said, "...when you see Jerusalem surrounded by armies then know its desolation is near."

Chapter Twenty-Eight
After The Great White Throne Judgment

Early this morning I was awakened by the Holy Spirit to get up and write. In only a matter of seconds He showed me what I was to write about. There seems to be some misunderstanding on what happens after the great white throne judgment as it is mentioned in Rev. 20.11-15. I will only quote verse 15 as a starting point for this commentary. "And anyone not found written in the Book of Life was cast into the lake of fire."

Now in Revelation 21.1 we address a new reality that has been misunderstood by many. It reads, "Now I saw a new heaven and a new earth, for the first heaven and the first earth had passed away. Also there was no more sea." What many of us have heard taught in the past is that this means our present earth will be renovated by fire and made new. This is incorrect.

When the verse says a new earth it doesn't mean from renovation by fire, it means an entirely new earth by a new act of creation. We know this from Isaiah 65.17. "For behold, I create new heavens and a new earth; and the former shall not be remembered or come to mind."Now going back to Rev. 21.1, we find more information about our present earth. It says it "passed away." The word "passed" in the Greek means it "departed" away. This indicates it actually departs from its present orbit and is given a different one. We also notice something else that as it departs it loses its sea and the reason for that is found in 2Peter 3.10. "...the heavens will pass away with a great noise, and the elements will melt with fervent heat; both the earth and the works that are in it will be burned up."

One of the reasons why there is a great noise at the earth's passing is the oceans are flashing into steam from the intense heat and is why John said "there was no more sea." Nothing is said about the new earth not having any sea or ocean only the present one. So does the new earth have any ocean? We don't know. The scripture doesn't tell us.

We come to an enigma found in Revelation 22.14-15 that many scholars avoid having to comment on. "Blessed are those who do His commandments that they may have the right to the tree of life, and may enter through the gates into the city. But outside are dogs and sorcerers and sexually immoral and murders and idolators and whoever loves and practices a lie."

Here's the enigma. How can these people be outside the city of the new Jerusalem, which is on the new earth if they were supposed to have been thrown into the lake of fire after the great white throne judgment on this present earth and then which departs from this orbit in a ball of fire?

The answer is found in what John meant by the use of the word "outside." This was a Christian term used by the early church to mean "outside the faith." We have examples of that. Colossians 4.5 says, "Walk in wisdom toward those who are outside, redeeming the time." 1Thessalonians 4.12 says, "that you may walk properly toward those who are outside..." And if you care to look it up, 1Timothy 3.7 is another reference.

John in Revelation 22 was just simply identifying who those are that are **"outside" the faith** that didn't make it, that didn't get translated to the new earth.

Chapter Twenty-Nine
Israel Living In Safety

Three times in Ezekiel 38 God declares that Israel will be living in safety (vv. 8, 11, 14) before Gog (i.e. Russia) wages war against them. No Scripture has failed to be fulfilled. Is Israel living in safety now? Since they are being threatened by their enemies all around them the answer to that question would have to be a no. The scripture actually quotes what Israel's enemies are saying about it right now in Psalm 83.4. "They have said, 'Come and let us cut them off from being a nation that the name of Israel may be remembered no more.'" Verse 5 goes on to say, "For they have consulted together with one consent; they form a confederacy against you."

It is interesting if you look at a Palestinian map of the middle east the nation of Israel isn't on it. Palestinians refuse to recognize that Israel is a nation but at the same time they want to be recognized in statehood.

The scripture in Psalm 83 goes on to list the names of the confederacy that are threatening Israel. For Israel to live in safety, as the scripture declares, it means these threats against Israel must be neutralized. Many attempts at peace negotiations have not worked and neither has giving up land for peace worked as the Gaza situation has proven. The only thing left is all out war. I believe the scripture is indicating there will be a major conflict involving these nations against Israel, and soon, and that these enemies will lose the conflict big time.

These nations that will be fighting against Israel listed in Psalm 83.6-8 are: Edom, the Ishmaelites, Moab, the Hagrites, Gebal, Ammon, Amalek, Philistia, Tyre and Assyria.

Edom is known today as southern Jordan; the Ishmaelites as Saudi Arabia; Moab as central Jordan; the Hagrites is Egypt; Gebal is northern Lebanon; Ammon is northern Jordan; Amalek is the Sinai; Philistia is Gaza; Tyre is southern Lebanon and Assyria is Syria.

It is important to list these names because it shows that Israel wins this war against them after which Israel can live in safety. So how does it show that? What we see is that Israel completely neutralizes the threat of these enemies because none of them are represented as fighting against Israel in the war depicted in Ezekiel 38 that occurs a few years later, and I'm sure they would if they could.

The warring factions against Israel in Ezekiel 38 are listed by name: Gog and Magog is Russia; Meshech and Tubal represent Moscow and Tobolsk; Gomer represents the eastern Europe and Armenian region; Togarmah is Turkey; Persia is represented as Iran, Iraq and Afghanistan according to Jewish commentaries; Ethiopia as Ethiopia; Libya as Libya.

So we see that none of the names listed in Psalm 83 are mentioned in Ezekiel 38 but yet in Ezekiel it says that Israel is found to be living in safety. This word "safety" has finger prints all over it of there having been a peace covenant agreed to giving all parties some guarantee of peace. Daniel 9.27 reveals that just such a peace covenant will be made for seven years and we know this happens at the beginning of the seven year tribulation time. So are we that close to the beginning of the tribulation time that the outcome of this next big conflict of Israel and the nations of Psalm 83 will bring about this seven year peace covenant? If we are, then how close must the rapture of the Church be? This would explain Jesus' statement in Matthew 24.44, "...the Son of Man is coming at an hour you do not expect."

I think the reason His coming will be at an hour most don't expect is because it will happen sooner than anyone expects.

Since this 1948 end-time generation is running out of time in which all these things are required to be fulfilled we know then that these things will need to happen soon. How close we must be!

Chapter Thirty
Understanding Revelation Chapter Twelve

The key to understanding chapter 12 is to understand the symbolism there. Most Bible teachers get the symbolism of verse one correct when they say the woman with the twelve stars represents Israel. But when they get to the male child of verse five they get it wrong by saying that this represents Jesus. So let's quote verse five. "She bore a male child who was to rule all nations with a rod of iron. And her child was caught up to God and His throne."

There are two things in particular that need to be noted. First of all, for the child to be Jesus the woman in verse one would have to be represented as Mary, not Israel, but she isn't. Mary has never been portrayed in scripture as being clothed with the sun, the moon under her feet and with a crown of twelve stars.

The next problem we have with the child being Jesus comes from verse four where the dragon stood ready to devour the child as soon as it was born. Yes, there was a threat on Jesus' life by king Herod but it wasn't as soon as Jesus was born but roughly two years later when the wise men arrived from the East to see Him.

The third problem with this child being Jesus is verse five says her child was caught up to God and His throne. Jesus was taken up into heaven after He finished His ministry but He most certainly wasn't a child when it happened. Neither was Jesus taken up into heaven in the middle of the tribulation as this child is. We know this because the woman who gave birth to the child flees into the wilderness (v.6) for "one thousand two hundred and sixty days" which remain of the tribulation time.

So the question is, who does this child represent then? To be consistent with the way this passage is being interpreted, if the woman, in the singular, represents a plurality of individuals then the child, in the singular also represents a plurality of individuals.

So who qualifies as the man child 3 1/2 years into the tribulation period? First, it must be recognized that the woman represents the religious non-Messianic Jews who flee into the wilderness and the birth of her child would be slated to have a religious upbringing. Previously, in chapter 11, we found the two witnesses in Israel witnessing. So the expected results of their witnessing would be converts, yes new believers, babes in Christ. And when did the two witnesses finish their ministry? Again it was finished at the midpoint of the tribulation period just prior to the man child being caught up to heaven. Who were their converts, these new believers in Christ? They were the 144,000 who are represented as the man child.

Chapter 14 confirms (vv.4-5) that they are caught up to God and to His throne as it said in Rev. 12.5. In chapter 14 they are in heaven just before the proclamation of the angel (vv.9-10) that those on earth are not to take the mark of the beast (not required until the last 3 1/2 years of the tribulation). This confirms the timing of the translation of the 144,000. Last of all, you can search from Genesis to Revelation and you won't find anyone else translated in the middle of the tribulation time; only the 144,000.

There is another lesser known error that is being propogated that needs to be addressed and can be resolved from Rev.12.9. First, I believe the scriptures lead us into truth and that the Bible does not lie to us. The error that is being propogated is believing the Devil and Satan are two different people.

103

Revelation 12.9 indicates the serpent of old is "called the Devil and Satan." To quote more of the verse it says, "So the great dragon was cast out, that serpent of old, called the Devil and Satan, who deceives the whole world; he was cast to the earth..." So if we were dealing with more than one entity here the verse would have read, and they were cast to the earth. But that isn't what the verse says; rather "he" was cast to the earth. This verse is giving the identity of the serpent in the garden who deceived Eve, calling the serpent by its other names - Devil and Satan. There is an even bigger error being propagated in that after Adam fell he became Satan. But again, in verse 9 the serpent who deceives is called Satan. So if the serpent was called Satan before he deceived Adam then how could Adam be Satan? We need to be in the Word so we aren't deceived by errors like this.

Chapter Thirty-One

Satan Becoming Frantic

In Revelation chapter 12 various names of Satan are used twelve times. Those names are: dragon, serpent, Devil, Satan and accuser of the brethren. Why not just use one name? I think it is because Satan is the master of disguise and this is the unmasking of the deceiver. When Satan wants to intimidate and to oppress and be vengeful he likes to disguise himself as a dragon. If he wants to be deceitful and cunning he will disguise himself as a serpent. But he can't fool God and when he comes before God he has to do so totally unmasked as Satan (Zech.3.1-2).

It is quite common in Scripture for the Lord to be telling of an event and then stop and go back and fill in on some of the details and this is what has happened in Revelation chapter 12. In verses 7-9 a war is described as taking place in heaven between Michael with his angels against Satan and his angels. It actually takes place before the dragon stands to devour the male child once the woman gives birth to it. We know this from v.13 which says, "Now when the dragon saw that he had been cast to the earth, he persecuted the woman who gave birth to the male child." Verse 14 indicates the woman flees into the wilderness where she will be for the last 3 1/2 years of the tribulation. In verse 15 the serpent reacts by spewing water out of his mouth like a flood hoping to overwhelm those fleeing.

The symbolism needs to be explained to see what is actually happening here. Spewing water out of his mouth means the order was given to give chase to those fleeing.

Water that would cause the woman to be carried away by the flood represents the antichrist's army in pursuit. A similar analogy has been given and explained in Isaiah 8.7. "Now therefore, behold, the Lord brings up over them the waters of the river, strong and mighty - the king of Assyria and all his glory; he will go up over all his channels and go over all his banks."

In Rev. 12.16 the woman is spared because it says, "the earth helped the woman and the earth opened its mouth and swallowed up the flood..." Yes, the earth literally opens up and swallows the antichrist's army, at least that contingent of forces that were given to him for this campaign (Daniel 8.12). There has been a precedent to this found in Numbers 16.31-33.

When Satan lost the heavenly battle the following statement was made, "Woe to the inhabitants of the earth and the sea! For the devil has come down to you, having great wrath, because he knows he has a short time." Then when the antichrist loses his army, verse 17 says, "And the dragon was enraged with the woman, and he went to make war with the rest of her offspring, who keep the commandments of God and have the testimony of Jesus Christ." These are the same ones who are spoken of in Daniel chapter seven just before the antichrist's kingdom is taken away from him. Verse 25 there says, "He shall speak pompous words against the Most High, shall persecute the saints of the Most High...then the saints shall be given into his hand for a time, and times and half a time."

Again, there is that last 3 1/2 year time period again and when it ends an angel binds Satan and throws him into the bottomless pit for 1,000 years (Rev. 20.1-3). So you can see why Satan is getting really nervous (frantic might be a better word) knowing his time is short.

106

These saints that the antichrist is moving to target next are all those people who got a wake-up call after the rapture of the Church took place. They are desperate to not face damnation so they are willing to do anything just to make it into God's kingdom. Psalm 50.5 tells how desperate they are. "Gather My saints together to Me, those who have made a covenant with Me by sacrifice."

These are a particular category of saint, i.e. only those who made a covenant with God through sacrifice. Those who became saints through obedience and belief in God's Word during the age of Grace, are not mentioned here. These saints in Daniel chapter seven and Rev. 12.17 are the same ones John needed help identifying in Rev. 7.14. So the angel told John, "These are the ones who come out of the great tribulation..." and this great harvest of souls are the ones represented in the harvest known as the Feast of Ingathering which takes place at the end of the year (Exodus 23.16).

Appendix I

Kings List Table

Reign of Solomon to Captives of Judah by Nebuchadnezzar.

Reference	King	Years Reigned	Reference
1Kings 11.42	Solomon	40 years	
1Kings 11.43	Rehoboam	17 years	1Kings 14.21
1Kings 15.2	Abijam	3 years	
1Kings 15.8	Asa	41 years	1Kings 15.10
1Kings 15.24	Jehosaphat	25 years	1Kings 22.42
2Chron. 21.1	Jehoram	8 years	2Chron. 21.5
2Kings 8.25	Ahaziah	1 year	2Kings 8.26
2Kings 11.2	Athaliah	6 years	2Kings 11.3
2Kings 11.21	Jehoash	40 years	2Kings 12.1
2Kings 14.1	Amaziah	29 years	2Kings 14.2
2Kings 14.21	Azariah	52 years	2Kings 15.2
2Kings 15.5	Jothan	16 years	2Kings 15.33
2Kings 15.38	Ahaz	16 years	2Kings 16.2
2Kings 16.20	Hezekiah	29 years	2Kings 18.2
2Kings 21.1	Manasseh	55 years	2Kings 21.1
2Kings 21.19	Amon	2 years	2Kings 21.19

Reference Index

Reference Index Continued

Reference Index Continued